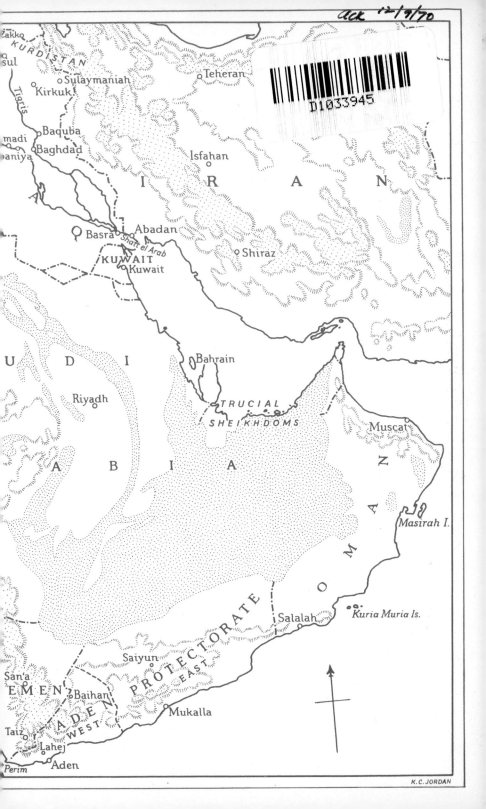

Zakko

KURDISTAN

sul

Tigris

madi
aniya

Sulaymaniah

Kirkuk

Baquba

Baghdad

Teheran

I   R   A   N

Isfahan

Basra

Abadan

Shatt el Arab

KUWAIT

Kuwait

Shiraz

U   D   I

Riyadh

Bahrain

TRUCIAL

SHEIKHDOMS

Muscat

A   B   I   A

O   M   A   N

Masirah I.

PROTECTORATE

EAST

Salalah

Kuria Muria Is.

Saiyun

San'a

EMEN

Baihan

ADEN

WEST

Mukalla

Taiz

Lahej

Perim

Aden

K.C.JORDAN

THE MIDDLE EAST IN REVOLUTION

THE
MIDDLE EAST
IN
REVOLUTION

HUMPHREY TREVELYAN

Gambit INCORPORATED
Boston
1970

To P.T.

CONTENTS

PREFACE

THIS is an account of events following three Arab revolutions, during the years when I lived with them, Egypt from August 1955 until the Suez affair in November 1956, Iraq from December 1958, four months after the revolution, until October 1961 after the failure of the Iraqi claim to Kuwait, and May to November 1967, the last days of the British in Aden.

This is sometimes regarded as a period of failure in British foreign policy in the Middle East. It should more properly be considered to have been a period of difficult readjustment to changing conditions in the Arab world and changing power relationships. Those who consider it to have been a period of failure, are the sentimentalists who do not understand why things should not have gone on as they were before. A more correct judgement is that though we made mistakes like everyone else involved, we have so far come through an unusually difficult and complex period without more damage to our real interests in the Middle East than was inevitable as a result of the fundamental changes in world conditions which have taken place since the end of the German war.

This is not a history of those times. It is no more than a personal record, based on accounts written, in each case, soon after the event, not on official papers nor on the accounts of others, which I have not read. If it is challenged on the grounds of inaccuracy or prejudice, I can only reply that this is how I remembered it when I came back, that I tried to be as objective as possible and that serious students can treat it as evidence to be accepted or rejected, as they please. People involved in events should not try and write their history, only material for history. In each part, it contains forewords of potted history for those wholly unfamiliar with the background, and brief accounts of what the scene looked like on arrival, the minimum necessary for the narrative to make sense. It is purely local in scope. It is not, for instance, directly concerned with the actions of the British, French, Israeli and American Governments leading up to the Suez affair, only with the impact of those actions upon events in Egypt. It is not concerned to commend or deplore British policy towards Iraq before the revolution, nor with the decision to withdraw from South Arabia, but only with the consequences in those countries.

The decisions and recommendations for which I was responsible, were the result of consultation among colleagues working daily together. I am grateful to them for the guidance and advice which so often stopped us going the wrong way, and to the colleagues in the Foreign Office who kept our end up at home. This book is as much their story as my own. We were not always right; that will be apparent from the narrative. None of us would claim more than an average score for judgement or foresight. The withdrawal from Aden was a political-military operation conducted jointly by Headquarters, Middle East and the High Commission. I do not believe that there could have been closer co-operation between Admiral Sir Michael LeFanu and his colleagues and us. I owe them a special debt of gratitude for their wisdom, their patience with me and their en-

couragement in bad times. My thanks are due to those
who have read the narrative of the events with which
they were concerned or extracts from it and have cor-
rected and improved it.

I have not been pedantically accurate in writing
Arab names. In the first part I have referred throughout to 'Nasser' without emotional overtones, since it
would be tedious to repeat every time his full name,
Gamal Abdul Nasser. I have similarly used 'Qasim'
in the second part, not Abdul Karim Qasim. I have
shortened Nuri es Said to Nuri Said, as the British
usually did. The point does not arise in the third part,
since in Aden we were dealing with a vacuum. There
are as few names of people and places mentioned as
possible. To most people they are only confusing.
Essential names of places are in the map.

CAIRO 1955-6

*Decisive action in the hour of need
Denotes the hero but does not succeed.*

Hilaire Belloc

O N 23 July 1952, the Society of Free Officers in the Egyptian army carried out a successful coup d'état and overthrew King Farouk. The movement was nominally led by General Mohammed Neguib, but was actually controlled by Colonel Nasser. The constitution was abolished and the country was ruled by a military oligarchy. In June 1953, a republic was declared with General Neguib as President and Prime Minister and Colonel Nasser as Deputy Prime Minister. A struggle for power developed between Neguib and Nasser and other contenders, from which Nasser emerged victorious in 1954. At the outset of the revolution, the leaders of the predominant political party, the Wafd, had been arrested and the party went into eclipse. In 1954 Nasser suppressed the communists. In October of that year the Muslim Brotherhood, an extreme religious organisation, attempted to kill Nasser and were also suppressed. Nasser was thus successful in consolidating his power.

In 1952 the revolutionary régime offered the Sudanese the right of self-determination. In February 1953 an Anglo-Egyptian agreement was signed providing for Sudanese independence after a three-year tran-

sitional period during which a constitution would be drafted and elections held under the supervision of an international commission.

During the first two years of the revolution, negotiations about the future of the Suez canal base were continued between Egypt and Britain. While the negotiations were deadlocked early in 1954, the Egyptian Government carried on guerrilla operations against the 70,000 British troops in the canal zone. By the end of May these operations were halted and an agreement was initialled at the end of July by which the British Government undertook to evacuate the Suez canal base by June 1956. The agreement provided that selected installations in the Base would be maintained for seven years by British civilian contractors, who would maintain and repair tanks, vehicles and other equipment belonging to the British Forces in the Middle East. A British firm was to occupy Abu Sueir airfield jointly with the Egyptian Air Force to provide a staging post for R.A.F. aircraft. The agreement was signed in October and in November an American-Egyptian agreement was signed for the grant of $40 millions aid.

I

O<small>N</small> 7 August 1955, I stepped out of an aeroplane
into the physical and political heat of Cairo. The impression which I had received in London was that the
great issues between Britain and Egypt had been solved
and that we were now in smoother waters, though
Egypt was, most unreasonably, still rocking the boat.
There was the Egyptian propaganda against the Baghdad Pact; there was the *Anshun* incident, when a
British steamer on the way to Aqaba was fired on by
the Egyptian Battery at the mouth of the Gulf. I was
instructed to point out to Nasser, as soon as I reasonably
could, that such conduct made it difficult for us to
meet the Egyptian requests for arms. For there were
many voices raised in the House of Commons to ask
why we should give Egypt so much help, when in return
we received abuse and disregard of our legitimate rights.
Was this in the spirit of the Agreement for the withdrawal of British troops, signed less than a year before,
the preamble of which foreshadowed a new era of firm
friendship and mutual understanding between the two
countries? It was a feeling of irritation, but not of any
real disquiet.

The Egyptians, we thought we knew from long experience, would always be difficult, but we were now

on a new and more favourable course. The 1954 Agreement was being satisfactorily carried out. The arguments over the Sudan were only minor irritations. There was always Palestine; but the uneasy peace had continued now for some years. There was hope for a settlement which we must actively pursue, and in the meanwhile our policy of balanced arms supplies to the Arabs and Israelis prevented either side from obtaining a decisive superiority over the other. Nor was it expected that the Soviet Union would take an active interest in Middle Eastern affairs. They had indeed issued a warning in terms familiar from Korea that they could not remain indifferent to the consequences of the Baghdad Pact; but this had not been followed up and was treated by the West as an outburst of pique against a Western diplomatic success, not as a portent of a new and dynamic Soviet policy towards the Arab world.

Beneath the surface the situation was much worse than was believed at the time. The honeymoon period of Anglo-Egyptian relations after the signature of the 1954 Agreement had lasted only a few months until early in 1955, when the advent of the Baghdad Pact had aroused powerful new resentments and suspicions in Nasser's mind and sharply diminished the chances of building a new relationship with him on the basis of the Agreement. The Israeli attack on Gaza in February, in Nasser's thinking, had radically transformed the Arab-Israeli situation and, with pressure for arms steadily increasing from the Egyptian Armed Forces, who were the main prop of the revolutionary régime, and with tempting Soviet offers to hand, Nasser was rapidly approaching the point at which he would be prepared to take major political risks in order to obtain a decisive superiority in armament over Israel. Meanwhile, Egyptian attempts to obtain control over the Sudan after the ending of the Condominium, were a fertile cause of misunderstandings between us. And so, on that hot August evening, I stepped out of my aeroplane into a situation which was far more threatening than was believed at home.

There were complications on both sides. Over the years Egypt had become a permanent strand in the substance of British politics and at this time was one of the most contentious British political issues. It was difficult for a Foreign Secretary to consider relations with Egypt objectively, when every decision on an Egyptian question exposed him to attack from one side or the other, when any action which could be represented as friendly to Egypt might be depicted in the Press by a cartoon of an exultant Nasser jumping in hob-nailed boots on the Foreign Secretary's cringing body, while, if he struck a tough attitude, he found it difficult to translate it into effective action, with most of the international pack against him. To the average Englishman Egypt had become the symbol of the decline of the British Empire, although it was never a part of the Empire, and the feeling of impotence and frustration natural in this period of transition, found expression in attacks on any Minister who could be represented as weak in dealing with Nasser.

The shadow of 1938 loomed large and a charge of appeasement of a dictator was the most serious danger to reputation and career. There was a wide divergence of views on our Middle Eastern policy. In the one view, Nasser had always been fundamentally opposed to British interests; we should never have treated him as anything but an enemy; the 1954 Agreement was lunacy and we should get nothing but trouble from it. In the other view, there was truth in the old saying that in the Middle East the British never saw the writing on the wall until they hit their heads against it; an attempt to hang on in occupation of Egypt would have led us into a real mess; our difficulties were due to our

inability to realise that we were not living in the
nineteenth century and no longer had the power to
enable us to keep the Middle East as our political
preserve.

We had to deal with a revolutionary situation, not
only in Egypt, but also in the rest of the Arab world.
The forces which Nasser sought to use were Arab
nationalism and the Arab social revolution. The forces
which came in his way were the perennial centrifugal
tendencies, the jealousies, the regional and historical
differences and the conflicts of interest in the Arab
world. The theoretical desire for Arab unity had to
contend with the jealousy between Iraq and Egypt, as
old as the time of Hammurabi and Senusret, with the
feud between Hashemite and Wahabi, with the com-
munal balance in the Lebanon, with the conflicting
interests of those who had the oil, the 'black gold', and
those who had not, with the numerous vested interests,
royal, political and commercial, which had grown since
the carving up of the Turkish Empire, and with the
suspicion that Nasser saw himself as on top of everyone
else. But, however much the other Arab Governments
disliked the idea of being run by the Egyptians, Nasser's
powerful radio propaganda, supported by the relative
strength of Egypt in the Arab world, was already making
Nasser into a symbol of Arab nationalism which none
dared ignore, and although Arab nationalism did not
bring Arab unity or even a united Arab foreign policy
or military command, it was a strong force and the
Arabs came together, if not always effectively, when
a general Arab interest was threatened, above all on
Palestine.

We were faced too by the social revolution at work
in the Arab world. The Egyptian revolution had been
successful because the rising lower-middle class, most
strongly represented in the Armed Forces, would no
longer put up with the exclusiveness and selfishness of

the old régime. The left wing had gained a measure of power in Syria and in 1955–6 was gaining strength in Jordan. The little States in the Gulf, so important to the West, were beginning to feel the ferment. Even the Iraqi oligarchy, ruling permanently under the form of continually changing Governments, were becoming nervous of the growing opposition to their exclusive control of affairs. Only the Wahabi Ruler of Saudi Arabia, supported by the tribal organisation of the State, remained relatively unaffected by the stirrings of the new classes in the Arab world.

The alignments in the Arab world were complicated and shifting, not simply the right against the left, the old against the new. The two poles were Iraq and Egypt. In between, politically and geographically, lay Saudi Arabia, Syria, Jordan and the Lebanon. In 1955–6 King Saud swung towards Egypt, being infected by Nasser's success, fearful of being pilloried as a bad Arab, a stooge of the imperialists, piqued by his inability through British opposition to appropriate Buraimi and perennially suspicious of the Hashemites' dormant pretensions to the Hejaz. Influenced by his Minister, Yusuf Yassin, hostile to the British since the accusations of bribery against him at the time of the Buraimi arbitration, Saud was temporarily in the Egyptian orbit and Saudi money used for political purposes, was a disturbing element.

In Syria, in which, as the Arabs say, everything grows, power was moving from the landlords to the left-wing politicians, who looked to the Egyptian revolution to support them, and Nasser was beginning to acquire the tempting position which caused him later to try and subsequently regret the experiment of Egyptian-Syrian union as a first step towards a United Arab Republic, in which the threads would be kept in Egyptian hands and of which only the name now survives. The Lebanon, precariously balancing its Muslim and Christian communities, kept itself apart, developing Beirut as the Paris of the Middle East, the safest home for the investment of oil royalties and the most convenient bolt-hole for Arab politicians in danger from their opponents at home. Jordan, a kingdom always about to fall apart but surviving miraculously until today, was entering a new and more dangerous phase of its existence, watched with covetous eyes by Syria, itself tempted by the glittering prospect of the 'Fertile Crescent' under Jordanian leadership, with British influence disappearing from the Legion which had been the main support of the Emirate, its border with Israel, formerly tranquil, now in danger of becoming the area of greatest tension. Here seemed to be the most probable scene of a clash between the old order and the new, between the revolutionary elements among the Palestinians of the West Bank supported by Nasser, and the young king, relying on the Beduins of Transjordan and the backing of his Hashemite cousins in Iraq.

The Middle East, like other parts of the new world emerging from past Empires, was an international jungle. Bribery, subversion, revolutionary conspiracy were common and no Government which had the means, was innocent of these expediencies in the conduct of international relations. A Syrian colleague, for instance, once complained to me that the Iraqis, then our allies, had failed to follow up their Syrian coups properly. He said that they had paid a large sum to instal a new Syrian Government, but had foolishly sat back and done nothing more. The Saudis had then bought the Government for a larger sum in their own interests and had followed this up by continuing to pay the right people.

It was an old saying in the Arab world that when two fish were fighting in the sea, the British were behind it, and, however innocent, the British and Americans were widely believed to be not wholly averse from some of the fashionable methods of influencing policy. We had certainly used these methods in both wars, when subversion in enemy occupied territory was considered a reputable occupation and funds were available for it. American views on what is justifiable in what might be termed 'the grey area in foreign relations' were stated by Mr Allen Dulles in his book on *The Craft of Intelligence* when he wrote 'In Iran a Mossadeq and in Guatemala an Arbenz came to power through the usual processes of Government and not by any Communist coup as in Czechoslovakia. Neither man at the time disclosed the intention of creating a Communist State. When this purpose became clear, support from outside was given to loyal anti-communist elements in the respective countries, in the one case to the Shah's supporters, in the other, to a group of Guatemalan patriots. In each case, the danger was successfully met . . . no invitation was extended by the *Government* in power for outside help.' Nasser has been singled out for attack for his subversive operations; but it would be a mistake, however much we deplore in principle this generally wasteful and inefficient method of conducting international affairs, to regard his actions as a black spot in an area of purity. They should be judged in the light of a climate of opinion which considered subversion and conspiracy as a normal method of governmental operation and only condemned it when it was unsuccessful.

This was the situation which we had to face. It was common sense for the Western Powers not to take any action which would bring the Arabs together in opposition to them. We could not ignore Arab nationalism. It was strongly backed by the Afro-Asian world, which regarded itself as the anti-colonial front, by the Communists intent on winning Arab friendship and, up to a point, by the Americans, mainly for historical and

sentimental reasons. The general trend of British policy
in bringing colonial territories to independence was to
put the nationalists into power and to make terms with
them. We had either to fight it successfully, which in
the long run we could not do, or to try and make such
terms with it as would safeguard our real interests
at a time when we had lost our old paramountcy in the
Arab world. We could still help our friends among the
old Arab Rulers and Sheikhs to resist subversion, being
careful not to embarrass them by policies which could
be represented as anti-Arab, while encouraging them,
without weakening their security, to introduce such
reforms in their territories as would ensure the support
of their people and deprive the extremists of the opportunity to exploit grievances. At the same time we had
to try and get on terms with the new Egypt. Nasser
might go, but the old Egypt would never come back.

The withdrawal of the British Forces radically transformed the situation in Egypt. Would it make everything easy, with the disappearance of Egypt's main
grievance against us, or would it merely increase Nasser's efforts to destroy our position elsewhere in the
Arab world? The Agreement was carried out without
any serious hitch. The last British soldier left Egypt a
few days before the final date fixed, the contractors
moved into position and local co-operation with the
Egyptian authorities, civil and military, was reasonably
good, very good with the Egyptian Air Force at Abu
Sueir.

By the middle of 1956, however, the basis on which
the Agreement rested had lost its validity and, even
before the Suez crisis, we in Cairo were considering
whether there was any sound reason to maintain the
Base for the agreed period. The Agreement provided
for the reactivation of the Base for defence against the
invasion of any Arab State or Turkey by a State other
than Israel. In effect, it provided that Egyptian terri-

tory could be used as a base for defence against Soviet attacks on the Middle East, and was, to that extent, an anti-Communist alliance, although there was no provision that Egypt should herself join in the military action contemplated. By the middle of 1956 the Agreement, though being punctiliously carried out, was really in ruins. The friendship foreshadowed in its preamble, had turned out to be something approaching hostility. The base for defence against the Soviet Union was situated in a country which was now receiving large quantities of Soviet arms and was remodelling its Forces and training methods on Russian lines. The climate had radically changed.

The argument of the right-wing critics of the British Government that the Agreement was a major mistake, since there had never been any hope of getting on terms with Nasser, implied that we could have kept British troops in Egypt indefinitely without serious political or military difficulty in the face of Egyptian and international opposition. In reality, evacuation was an inevitable retreat in the face of Egyptian nationalism, which grew stronger as our power in the world diminished. We did not take our Forces away from Egypt in order to strengthen our position in the Middle East, nor out of any excessive expectation of fruitful anti-Communist co-operation with Nasser, though we may have persuaded ourselves that this was a possible outcome of our action. We took them away because we could not keep them there much longer. We were only retreating from positions which had already been lost.

Getting on terms with Egypt could not mean giving way to Nasser's ambitions where they conflicted with our interests. These were still great throughout the Middle East; the oil, the maintenance of communications to the East by sea and air, the strengthening of the weak countries on the southern border of the Soviet Union, our position in South Arabia and the Gulf, our responsibilities to the Sudan, the maintenance of the Arab-Israeli truce until the Israelis abandoned their ambition to expand further into Arab lands and the Arabs their ambition to drive the Israelis into the sea. It was not going to be easy. The young Egyptian revolutionaries, fresh from their success in getting rid of the British after seventy-five years of occupation, were still obsessed by the past, still suspicious that the British would somehow get back again, not yet confident in their new independence. There were still relics of the past in the Suez Canal Company, the presence of British on the Canal, the dependence on the West for arms.

Nasser's dreams were bound to bring him into conflict with us. The British were still under the illusion that, even after the withdrawal from Egypt, they could organise the Arab world in their interests against Egyptian opposition. The Arab-Israeli frontier had become far more dangerous with the removal of British Forces from the Egyptian lines of communication and the weakening of British influence in Jordan. What was needed was a period of quiet on both sides. What happened was that both we and Nasser pressed the other to give way. Nasser failed to see that his ambitions exceeded his strength. Our actions were designed for a situation which no longer existed.

important element in their policy. Besides the obvious Egyptian interest in the Nile valley as a whole, control of the Sudan would be a first step towards achieving a dominant position in North Africa.

The Egyptians tried to get what they wanted by pressure, including bribery. By August 1955 this was beginning to look a bad bet. The Sudanese Ministers had tasted power and saw their way to independence. They had no intention of submitting to Egyptian domination. Azhari, the Prime Minister, had broken with the Egyptians and had become a strong opponent of the Egyptian line. The Egyptians had overplayed their hand. Sudanese affairs were in the hands of Major Salah Salem. While he was in charge, it was the only current political question on which Nasser seemed unwilling to give his views off the cuff. Later, Nasser told me that he had always been against bribery in the Sudan, since you could not hope to conduct policy by bribery. For the people bribed were only interested in the money, not in the policy. I told him the current story that coffins which were supposed to contain the bodies of Sudanese dying in Cairo, were sent to Khartoum by air, and that on one occasion the coffin was so full of silver that it needed thirty men to carry it off the airport. Nasser laughed, but said nothing.

The Egyptians tried also to use the sects, the Ansar and the Khatmia, against the politicians, but failed there too. In any case, the power of the sects was waning and the politicians represented the rising nationalist forces in the Sudan, just as much as the Egyptian revolution represented those same forces in Egypt. Sudanese nationalism was too strong. The Egyptians had no hope of getting a link which implied subordination of the Sudan to Egypt. That position had been lost with the signature of the Sudan Agreement and could not be recovered. The most that they could have obtained would have been a formal recognition of a common interest in the Nile waters and the establishment of technical agencies for their regulation and development. Egyptian methods were clumsy and their bribery and interference brought them only the hostility and unification of the Sudanese factions and sects against them.

In my first few days I received instructions to speak to Nasser about his propaganda directed to the Sudan, and at his suggestion I gave him the message when I presented my credentials. At a subsequent meeting with Nasser and Salah Salem, they admitted their propaganda, justifying it by saying that it was in reply to Azhari who was suppressing public expression of the Egyptian point of view and using the Sudanese broadcasting system to put his own views across. Azhari could not be expected to do anything else, and it was hardly surprising that the Egyptians answered him with their propaganda about the unity of the Nile valley and the need for the link. It was all very well for us to say that we were scrupulously independent, while our partners in the Condominium were not. We had no vital interest in the Sudan, whereas the Nile valley was the basis of life in Egypt. We wanted to keep the Egyptians out of the Sudan and it suited us that Azhari should broadcast his views and that the Egyptians should not broadcast theirs.

At the end of August mutiny broke out in the Southern Sudan. There was an old tradition in the South of fear of the Arab North, with its slaving history. The South had remained very much on its own during the Condominium and had developed separatist tendencies. When the British district officers were withdrawn, the South was left to the administration of the Sudanese Government, the members of which were predominantly Northerners. The Southerners felt that they had been betrayed to their old enemies. Salah Salem was right when he said that the Egyptians could not have created the mutiny, but they had certainly encouraged it. Egyptian propaganda and money had for some time been employed by the Egyptian irrigation officials stationed under old arrangements to watch the level of the Nile. The Egyptians presumably calculated that the Southerners could be brought to regard the Egyptians as their supporters against the North and that revolt in the South could bring about the fall of Azhari. Saleh Salem appeared to know what was going on before the Governor-General was aware of it. He visited me late one evening in a state of great excitement to propose the despatch of British and Egyptian troops to the South. It looked as if the plan was for the British troops to move out in due course and for the Egyptian troops to stay and restore the crumbling Egyptian position. We did not respond. The Sudanese Government showed themselves surprisingly competent in dealing with the situation and Salah Salem's last effort failed. This was his political eclipse. Nasser took the opportunity to get rid of him from the Council of the Revolution, though retaining a personal affection for his old comrade.

The British and Egyptian Forces left the Sudan on schedule. The next step under the Agreement was to organise the election of the Constituent Assembly under the supervision of an International Commission. Discussions between us and the Egyptians on the constitution of this Commission had reached deadlock when I arrived, mainly on the Egyptian proposal to include in it representatives of the Condominium Powers and Czechoslovakia. The only way out was to by-pass the difficulty. The choice of the Commission was therefore left to the Sudanese Parliament which supported the Egyptians in the inclusion of the Czechs and us in the exclusion of the Condominium Powers. It went further. Under the influence of Syed Ali Mirghani, head of the Khatmia sect, it voted that there should be a plebiscite to decide between independence and a link with Egypt, instead of the question being decided by the Constituent Assembly, as provided in the Agreement. Neither of the Condominium Powers wanted to put themselves in the position of opposing the vote of the Sudanese Parliament. They therefore accepted this vote as an amendment to the Agreement, although it seemed highly unlikely that a plebiscite could ever be organised, particularly in the disordered conditions in the South.

After Salah Salem's disappearance I had to deal with Nasser on the Sudan. Salah Salem had invariably given his version of our talks to the Press. Nasser agreed that we should keep our talks confidential and should not 'put each other in a corner'. If this could be achieved, we should have a better chance of getting through our difficulties. I now had to get his views on specific proposals for the establishment of the Commission, which would have to supervise the plebiscite as well as the election of the Constituent Assembly. For six weeks Nasser stalled and gave no answer. I waited for his next move.

The move came from our side. The Governor-General, Sir Knox Helm, decided that the situation in the Sudan was getting out of control and that his position after the withdrawal of the British contingent, would rapidly become impossible. He was right. The drafters of the Sudan Agreement had not been realistic. The Agreement provided for a long and complicated process leading to independence. The foreign civil servants and Forces were to leave. Commissions were to be established to guide the Governor-General, to supervise Sudanisation of the Civil Service, to organise the elections and to supervise the formation and work of the Constituent Assembly. Only when the Constituent Assembly had drafted the new Constitution and elections to a new Parliament had been held, was the Condominium to come to an end and the Governor-General to be replaced by the first President. But there was little prospect of this procedure being carried through to the end in this way long after the Forces of the Condominium States had been withdrawn from the country. At some stage the Sudanese were going to take matters into their own hands and the Governor-General would have to go. He now proposed that the two Condominium Powers should immediately declare the Sudan independent and the Agreement and Condominium abrogated. On instructions I put this proposal to Nasser. He replied that he was now convinced that if there were a free vote in the Sudan, the Sudanese would vote overwhelmingly for independence and separation from Egypt. However, for internal reasons, he was not prepared to admit this publicly, as he would be doing if he agreed with our proposal. It would have been awkward for him to have to admit defeat in this way. He may also have thought that the tide could suddenly turn again and that his best chance was to keep the Condominium going for as long as possible.

My interest was to maintain a logically consistent position, which I could support. We had made an agreement with Egypt over the Sudan. We and the Egyptians were committed to carry it out together and amendments could only be made by agreement. Nasser had not agreed to our proposal for amendment. We must therefore revert to the Agreement, and continue to discuss with the Egyptians what amendments it needed in the light of the practical situation. The British Government and the Governor-General naturally took a different view. They were determined that Sudanese independence must be brought on quickly in order to defeat Egyptian manoeuvres and demonstrate in the Sudan that the British were the real architects of Sudanese independence. We owed the Egyptians nothing in the way of fair treatment. They had tried to twist the Agreement, to buy the Sudanese, to claim every development favourable to the Sudanese as their own inspiration and to represent themselves as the defenders of Arab nationalism against British imperialist designs. They had cheated all along, as most Governments would have in their position. But I doubted whether we should be well advised to adopt the same sort of tactics, if only because we should probably be defeated by the Egyptians in a game of this sort.

With the Governor-General's support, the Foreign Office proposed that we should unilaterally declare the Sudan independent and the Condominium no longer in existence. I commented that this would be regarded in Egypt as a breach of the Sudan Agreement and that we must accept the risk, in return, of an Egyptian denunciation of the 1954 Agreement on the Suez Canal Base. (It would at least have encouraged them to break the Base Agreement once the British troops had left.) The Foreign Office disclaimed the interpretation which we in Cairo had unhesitatingly put on their proposal, but dropped it. It was followed by a new suggestion, also supported by the Governor-General, that he should go to the Sudanese Prime Minister, suggest that he should make a declaration of independence and promise the British Government's support if he did so. We protested against this. We assumed that the Egyptians had an agent in the Sudanese Prime Minister's office and that it was impossible for the Governor-General to make any move without its being immediately known to the Egyptians. I had an understanding, whatever its value, with Nasser that we should not 'put each other in a corner' and I did not want to be the first to break it by going behind his back in a way which would quickly become known to him. The Foreign Office's reply opened with the sentence: 'I quite understand your position, but in life one must play the cards as they fall.' In Cairo we thought that that was all right provided you were sure you had the highest trump in your hand.

The Governor-General was instructed to speak to Azhari and I was told to stall. Azhari was non-committal. Nasser knew at once what had happened. He went over to the attack. Having decided correctly that I was trying to cheat him, he would no longer see me on Sudanese affairs, which were now put into the charge of Colonel Zachariya Mohieddin, the Minister of the Interior. Egyptian propaganda to the Sudan and attacks against us had died down. Now the propaganda began again, supported by an official Note which accused us of deliberately holding up the constitution of the International Commission and thus the procedure leading to Sudanese independence, and which ignored the fact that I had been pressing Nasser for weeks to get on with setting up the Commission and that he had been responsible for nearly all the delay.

The British Government were now determined to stall on the Commission until Azhari had had every opportunity to make his declaration. It seemed likely that by the end of October he would be able to get a vote in favour of independence through the Sudanese Parliament. I was therefore instructed to tell the Egyptians that we understood that the Sudanese Parliament would probably pass a resolution in two weeks' time which would again completely transform the situation. The Condominium Powers were no longer in a position to dictate to the Sudanese Parliament and would have to fall in with their ideas. It would be prudent therefore to wait until we saw the result of this expected move.

The Egyptians now pursued two lines of attack. They pointed to an exchange of letters attached to the Sudan Agreement which provided that the International Commission should decide who should be the Commander-in-Chief after the departure of the British and Egyptian contingents. The exchange of letters had been agreed on in default of agreement on the substantive point. They argued that by refusing to set up the Commission, we were preventing this point being settled. The Governor-General's powers as Commander-in-Chief would lapse in a week or two when the troops finally left; there would be no Commander-in-Chief and we should be in breach of the Agreement. I argued in reply that in default of a new appointment the Governor-General would retain his powers and that the normal way of construing the exchange of letters would be that, if the International Commission should not be able to make its decision by the date contemplated in the Agreement, they should make it at the earliest practicable date, the existing situation continuing until they had done so. The Egyptians then issued a Note to the Powers selected by the Sudanese Parliament as members of the International Commission, asking them to nominate their representatives on the Commission. Czechoslovakia did so. The others held their hand. At the end of the month we heard that Azhari was not going to put anything to the Sudanese Parliament, since he could not get the agreement of all the factions. For the moment therefore the Governor-General's manoeuvre was defeated and the British Government had no alternative but to revert to the letter of the Agreement.

We had changed positions with the Egyptians once and now both sides reverted to their old positions. We had pressed for progress under the Agreement and they had delayed. Then we had asked for delay and they had pressed. Now we pressed again and they stalled. We said that, since the Sudanese Parliament were not now intending any new move, we were ready to make supplementary agreements providing for the plebiscite and for the establishment of the Commission. They argued that as soon as the plebiscite was taken, the Governor-

General must disappear, that the Condominium would then have terminated and that the remainder of the steps leading to independence should continue to be supervised by the Commission. We judged that their idea was to continue their interference in the Sudan directly and through the Czech member of the Commission in the absence of a British Governor-General in a position to block their intrigues and to intrigue against them. We refused to accept this as a valid interpretation of the Agreement. The Governor-General had to stay and the Condominium to continue until independence, and the Commission which derived its existence from the Condominium, must be dissolved on its termination. After some argument the Egyptians dropped their new line and we were back on the Agreement as modified by the decision to have a plebiscite. The amendments to the Agreement were signed on 10 December.

We were now in the last phase. The Governor-General was determined to get out of his uncomfortable position. On his initiative I was instructed to propose that the British Governor-General should be withdrawn and a neutral, such as a Swede, appointed. The Egyptians reacted, as usual, by sniffing around to find out what new trick we were up to. Meanwhile, Sir Knox Helm was anxious to take leave in England over Christmas, since his annual leave had been interrupted by the mutiny in the South and his son was about to leave for West Africa. Azhari agreed and Sir Knox assured the British Government that no important developments were to be expected during his absence. He left for England. No sooner was he out of the way than Azhari, with the agreement of the Sudanese Parliament, declared that Sudanese independence was a fact and would date formally from 1 January 1956.

This time we succeeded in acting jointly with the Egyptians. Both recognised that there was nothing

either could do about it and agreed on a joint statement and joint arrangements for terminating the
consortium. Sir Knox Helm never returned. The
Egyptians simultaneously and inconsistently alleged
that it was all a British plot, Sir Knox Helm's sudden
departure having been arranged in order to leave
Azhari free to make his move, and that Egypt was the
maker of the independent Sudan. Major Salah Salem
was invited by the Sudanese Government to spend a
few days in Khartoum. The Egyptians may have known
all about it beforehand, but they had lost and the
Sudanese and British had got their way. The Sudanese
were able to start their life as an independent State
with fair prospects. We and the Egyptians had intrigued
against each other and confidence was further eroded.
I was naturally concerned with the effect of all this
manoeuvring on Anglo-Egyptian relations and felt that
we could have arrived at the same result with less
damage to them if we had taken things more quietly.
But it can equally be argued that the damage was worth
the result and that at least it showed the Egyptians that
they could not always get their own way.

3

In August 1955, the Americans lost their opportunity to arm the Egyptian Forces. Up till then, the Egyptians had obtained most of their arms and their military, naval and air training from the British. Western policy was to maintain a rough balance between the Arabs and the Israelis and to limit the flow of arms into the Middle East. During the Arab-Israeli war of 1948 the Security Council had imposed an arms embargo, but both sides had acquired a miscellaneous collection of arms from various sources. Later, during the period of undeclared hostilities between the Egyptians and the British Forces in Egypt, we had imposed another embargo on the supply of arms to Egypt, which, through the machinery of tripartite consultation in Washington, was adhered to by the Americans and the French. The Egyptians had however received a fair amount of supplies from other sources throughout this period. After the signature of the Anglo-Egyptian Agreement of October 1954, the ban was lifted and the Egyptians received substantial supplies of arms from us during the first half of 1955, including 32 Centurion tanks and two destroyers which were fitted out in the summer of 1956.

This supply ran into political difficulties in 1955, as a result of Egyptian propaganda against us in other Arab countries, the attack on the British steamer in the straits

of Tiran and the continued tension on the Israeli-
Egyptian frontier. We told the Egyptians that these
difficulties were of their own making. They chose to
regard them as the imposition of political conditions.
They had some reasonable grounds for complaint. As a
result of an undertaking given in the House of
Commons by the Minister of State, no ammunition
could be delivered directly from the Suez Canal Base
to the Egyptian Forces. Material which it had been
agreed should be supplied and stocks of which were
in the Base, had to be shipped to England and fresh
material sent from England. Twenty-five pounder guns
were supplied, but no ammunition for them. Obsolete
Sea Furies were held up for months for no apparent
reason. In June the Egyptians complained that their
Quartermaster-General on a visit to London had been
insulted and lectured in the Foreign Office. The
Egyptians objected to the Western policy on the ground
that it meant balancing the arms supply between Israel
and the Arab States as a whole and that, if there were
to be a balance, it should be in proportion to population.
We rejected this as absurd; we intended no precise
balance; we supplied each State with what we
considered necessary for their defence. By the middle of
1955 the Egyptians had probably decided that they
would not get anywhere near what they wanted from
us.

At the same time, they were negotiating with the
Americans. In 1954 the Americans had offered military
aid, subject to their usual conditions, which included
the acceptance of a military mission. Nasser had refused
this offer on the ground that the conditions were
politically unacceptable. Negotiations had then started
for the purchase of American arms. A programme for
the supply of arms to the value of £27 million was
agreed. Nasser said that his resources in dollars were
exactly the required amount and that he could not

spend all his dollars on arms. He wanted to pay in Egyptian currency. The Americans could have found a way round this difficulty, but they did not seem to realise in Washington that the matter was urgent and important, or perhaps, as I have heard suggested, it was realised at a late stage that the sale of arms to Egypt was politically impossible and the negotiations were therefore allowed to founder. They remained dormant for months and Nasser lost patience.

Meanwhile, in the spring, the Russians had made a general offer to supply arms against Egyptian cotton and sterling. There is some evidence that at the 'summit' Conference at Geneva in July the Russians were encouraged by the lack of strong Western reaction to their hints of commercial sales of arms to the Middle East. Nasser would probably have still preferred to get arms from the West, as he said, and used the Russian offer to try and push the American deal to a conclusion. In June he told the American Ambassador, Mr Byroade, that he had an offer from the Russians and would accept it if he could not get the American arms. Mr Byroade told my predecessor, Sir Ralph Stevenson, who reported to London. He received immediate instructions to warn Nasser that if he took arms from the Russians, he would get no more from us and would be making a gift to Israeli propaganda. This message infuriated Nasser. He described it to me later as a threat which he could not accept, and told me that from that moment he had determined to have no more conversations with the British about arms. He upbraided Mr Byroade for having passed on what he had said to Sir Ralph Stevenson.

In the middle of August, Mr Byroade told me about the American-Egyptian arms negotiations. He realised that this was a matter which would have far-reaching effects on future Egyptian policy and alignment, and did not discount Nasser's threat to take Russian arms.

We had previously tried to keep the supply of arms to Egypt in British hands. In the new circumstances that no longer made sense. As the days passed and no answer came from Washington, Mr Byroade became increasingly worried and the rumours about Russian arms became more frequent and circumstantial. It appears from subsequent statements by Nasser that the decision to take Russian arms was reached at the end of August. The dangers of the situation were not grasped in London either.

At about this time, as a result of a fresh outbreak of fighting on the Israel border, the British Government proposed a tripartite arms embargo which would not be declared, and themselves held up all supplies to Israel and Egypt. I telegraphed that this would not lessen tension on the border and that the possibility of the Egyptians taking Russian arms must not be discounted. The Foreign Office were acting as if the Egyptians could still only look to the West for arms and they could use their position as monopoly supplier to put on political pressure. General Hakim Amer, the Commander-in-Chief, now told us that he would not after all be able to accept an invitation from the Chief of the Imperial General Staff to him to visit the British Forces in Germany and the United Kingdom. This was an ominous sign. Amer told me later that the reason was the decision to take Russian arms. The Americans were being urged by the Egyptian Ambassador in Washington to clinch the Egyptian-American deal before it was too late.

In the last week of September the Russian arms deal seemed certain and I could have no further doubt after a conversation with Amer. On the next day, 27 September, I was instructed by the Foreign Office to ask Nasser for the facts. I called on him at the office of the Revolutionary Council, where, as I learnt afterwards, he was entertaining two Americans, not members of the Embassy. He told me that he had made an agreement with the Russians for the supply of arms.

The next morning, the Foreign Office spokesman told the British Press. I felt that, if it was decided that we should make this information public, I should at least have been told to inform Nasser. He was incensed and again considered that we had put him 'in a corner'. The next evening he announced in a violent speech at the opening of an Armed Forces' exhibition that the Egyptian Government had signed a contract with Czechoslovakia for the purchase of arms. Nasser admitted to me afterwards that he had told me they were Russian arms, though he said he had also mentioned that Egyptian experts had been in 'Brag', which he pronounced with a short 'a'. It was of course a deal with the Russians and the Czechs only came into it at the last moment as a front for political reasons. The idea of representing it as a Czech deal was perhaps that it would sound better that way, since Israel had had considerable arms supplies from the Czechs. My report, even if it was not complete owing to my misunderstanding what Nasser said, gave the truth of the matter.

The storm broke, with headlines in the Press, emotional messages across the Atlantic, instructions to me to remonstrate with Nasser and the despatch to Cairo of a special American envoy, Mr George Allen, then Assistant Secretary for Middle Eastern Affairs in the State Department. I saw Nasser twice. I told him on instructions of the serious concern of the British Government and warned him of the dangers involved in an arms race with Israel and in buying arms from the Communists, with the dependence on them which this must entail, for spare parts, replacements, training and technicians. We had more conversations in subsequent weeks. At this stage there was no chance that they would have any effect. We had lost our opportunity in the early summer.

Nasser's consistent line was that the basic situation had been changed by the Israeli attack of February 1955. He said that since that date he had been increasingly nervous of Israeli intentions. The Israelis were far better armed than the Egyptians and were in the process of gaining a decisive superiority. He quoted a French pamphlet which he insisted was derived from official sources, which gave a list of arms supplied to the Israelis by the British. He printed an extract from a British military intelligence review which his agents had stolen from a British Unit in the Canal Zone, in order to support his claim that the Israelis had arms superiority even over the Arabs as a whole. He enlarged on the pressure continually coming from his younger officers, who had been urging him for months to accept the Soviet offer and thus redress the balance. He put the blame on us and the Americans for our failure to give him enough arms and for our political conditions. He spoke of his sleepless nights and increasing tension. He had no alternative. This was only a one-shot affair. He had ordered spares of one third the value of the arms. He knew the dangers well and would guard against them. He did not intend to get rid of the British only to bring in the Russians. In any case, it was for him to decide where he should get his arms and he was breaking no agreement by getting them from the Communists. I replied that he under-rated the danger of an arms race and of Communist infiltration, that his information about our arms supplies to Israel was not true – the French pamphlet, for instance, was not official and was nonsense – and that even if he were not breaking any agreement, he was certainly not acting in the spirit of the preamble of the Base Agreement, which contemplated the development of friendly relations between us after the end of the occupation.

The Americans' despatch of Mr George Allen from Washington, whatever the original reason for it, suggested a tough American attitude, but there was no effective action which they could take. The State Department had put it out that he was on a normal parochial tour which would include Athens, but this caused a violent reaction in Athens at that moment of resentment against American policy on Cyprus. He arrived with a written message from Mr Dulles, which hinted at retaliatory measures. Mr Allen read the message to Nasser, but wisely did not leave the text with him, since Nasser could have used it effectively against the Americans to consolidate support for him in Egypt. Mr Allen's interviews were difficult and he left without having made any impression on Nasser, who was in no position to change his decision, particularly after the publicity which had involved his prestige.

We heard later that when the news of the despatch of an American envoy reached Cairo, Nasser had been urged at a stormy meeting of the Revolutionary Council to break off American-Egyptian relations and organise demonstrations against the American Embassy, but had wisely refused. On 26 July 1956, in the speech at Alexandria in which he announced the nationalisation of the Suez Canal Company, Nasser said that just before Mr Allen's arrival, an American official had told him that he should not take Mr Dulles's message too seriously. According to an American account, what really happened was that the news of Mr George Allen's mission reached Nasser before it became public, as a result of a leak from Washington. He was seeing one of his American friends that evening and threatened an immediate row. He was calmed down and advised to wait and see what Mr Allen said before making a row about it. It was sensible advice. In any case, this conversation can have made no difference to Nasser's reaction. He had made his deal and could not go back on it. He was on strong ground and he knew it. Nasser must have made his plans on the assumption that he would get no more arms from us. He had got our agreement to end the occupation. He had broken no agreement himself. He had presumably decided that he was not going to get any arms from the Americans. He was prepared to risk Western hostility in order to get the arms he urgently wanted to satisfy his officers and catch up with the Israelis.

Nasser's action strengthened his position inside Egypt and in the Arab world. He imposed a 'voluntary' levy to help pay for the arms, the victims of which included Government officials, businessmen needing Government good-will and some sublimely unaware American Senators who contributed in Nasser's ante-room to what they imagined to be a charitable cause, which the *New York Times* obligingly told their Jewish constituents was a levy to fight Israel. He could get what he wanted from the Soviet Union without completely breaking with the West and could play both sides, if he did not overplay his hand. We did not believe his statement that this was a 'one-shot' deal. It was presumably a basic agreement which would cover successive orders. By the middle of 1956 the Egyptians had probably acquired from the Communists about 50 I.L.28s, 100 MIGs, 300 medium and heavy tanks, more than a hundred self-propelled guns, 200 armoured personnel carriers, two destroyers, four minesweepers, twenty motor torpedo boats, five hundred pieces of artillery, rocket launchers, bazookas, plastic mines, small arms, radar, wireless equipment, small boats, etc. Two submarines were delivered in 1957. The value of the equipment delivered by the middle of 1956 was probably about £150 million.

Nasser had established commercial relations with Communist China, but still recognised the Nationalists and there was a Chinese Nationalist Ambassador in Cairo. In the spring of 1956 he suddenly recognised

Peking.

We could not understand why he had done it at that moment, since we heard that it was on the eve of a debate in the American Congress on a Bill which would give authority for the sale of American cotton surpluses abroad, decrease the import quota for Egyptian cotton and add two types of cotton exported by Egypt to the list of types restricted by this quota. We were told that Senator Knowland, a strong supporter of Chiang Kai-shek, had promised to sponsor an amendment in Egyptian interests, but had withdrawn his promise after Nasser's action and the consequent adverse comment in the United States. We did not know whether this account was accurate, but in any case it was difficult to explain Nasser's hasty action. I asked him later about it. He told me that he had heard from his Intelligence that during the visit of Bulganin and Khrushchev to London, Sir Anthony Eden had proposed a United Nations arms embargo in the Middle East. He had been advised that the Russians could not oppose this proposal, which was likely to be confirmed by the United Nations and that therefore he should recognise Communist China in order to enable him to get arms through the Chinese and thus circumvent the embargo. I had confirmation of this story from another source, according to which the advice came from the Russians. Actually, Sir Anthony Eden had only proposed restraint in the supply of arms to the Middle East. An arms embargo which would prevent the supply of American arms to Israel and American and British arms to members of the Baghdad Pact was of course never in the slightest degree likely, but the story which Nasser told me seemed to make sense. It is difficult to see any other reason for his recognition of Communist China at that moment.

By 1956 the Communists were taking a substantial percentage of the Egyptian cotton crop. They could give high prices for it under a barter deal in exchange for obsolescent arms. They received orders for the supply of industrial equipment and for the erection of factories, and loans for industrial development were discussed. They were active in the cultural field and could be relied on to give political support on every international issue, especially an Arab-Israeli issue. In March 1956, Nasser told Anthony Head, then Minister of Defence, that he was aware of the danger of getting into a position like that of Yugoslavia in 1948. He had therefore imposed a limit on trade with the Communists; what he called his safety catch. But it seemed to us, as time went on, that the safety catch was off most of the time, though I believed throughout that he did not intend to fall completely into Communist hands. The Russians wisely did not push too hard. They allowed him to suppress the local Communist party and to put many Egyptian Communists in prison. In return, the Egyptian Press were ordered not to criticise the Russians. Egyptian politics were now in a completely new setting.

4

Nasser took a cautious line with us on Israel. He said that up till February 1955 he had felt that there was a reasonable chance of peace. After the Israeli attack on the Egyptian Headquarters in Gaza a few weeks after Ben Gurion had come back to power, he had been in constant fear of an Israeli attack, tension had increased and the chances of a settlement had almost disappeared. It could only again become possible, he said, if tension again diminished, and this might take a long time. In the event, tension on the border steadily increased until the Israeli attack in October 1956.

Israeli policy was to maintain moral superiority on the border at all costs. They retaliated with interest for each Arab assault. They knew the risks involved in the short term, but accepted them as necessary if they were to assure their security. Up till September 1955, most of the incidents occurred in and around the Gaza strip. Nasser said that he had few regular Forces beyond the Southern end of the strip, which was garrisoned principally by the National Guard and the Palestine refugees who formed the nucleus of a Palestine army in exile. He said that he had made these dispositions because of the danger that troops in the strip would be cut off by an Israeli attack to the South. On the Egyptian side of the line there was a fairly large population, mainly refugees from Palestine, who looked with bitter feelings over the border at the lands and homes which they had lost. On the Israeli side there were one or two settlements (kibbutzim) a few kilometres from the border, but apart from them, only desert. The Egyptian defence was therefore mainly from fixed posts and the Israeli defence by mobile patrols.

From time to time, the Israelis deliberately provoked the Egyptians. They would drive their armoured vehicles almost up to the Egyptian posts, shouting insults at the men manning them. The Egyptians would lose their tempers as they were meant to, and shoot. The Israelis would promptly bring up a Force which they had in readiness and wipe out the Egyptian post. The border was only partly demarcated and there were no obstacles on it. Nasser wanted the Forces on both sides to withdraw, on the ground that the only way of stopping these incidents was to keep the soldiers out of sight of each other. The Israelis wanted to demarcate the border with barbed wire. The Egyptians, suspicious of anything tending to give the border the status of a permanent frontier, would only agree to the erection of obstacles by each side in their own territory, coupled with a withdrawal of both Forces. The Israelis wanted incidents to be discussed directly between the Israeli and Egyptian Commanders of the sector. The Egyptians rejected this as tending to imply a recognition of the State of Israel. By August 1955 there was deadlock.

At the end of August there was very nearly a major clash. The Israelis probably started it. Each side retaliated in turn. The Egyptians sent their commandos (fedayeen) to attack civilians and installations deep inside Israeli territory. Their excuse was that this was the only form of retaliation within their power, owing to the absence of objectives which their regular Forces could reach near the border. The Israelis retaliated by attacking the commando training centre at Khan Yunus in the Gaza strip. At a most dangerous moment in this series of incidents, information was received that the Egyptians were going to attack again, in answer to the last Israeli attack. They were urged to show restraint. Whether they had made a firm decision to attack I do not know. No attack took place and General Burns, the United Nations representative, succeeded in negotiating a cease-fire. Perhaps it would have been better if the major clash had occurred at this time and not fourteen months later.

In September the Israelis occupied the demilitarised zone of El Auja in contravention of the terms of the armistice. On 2 October both sides withdrew from their positions in the zone at General Burns's request; but incidents continued in this sector of the border. The Israelis soon reoccupied the zone. On 28 October they attacked deep into Egyptian territory in this area and on 3 November took a hill partly inside the zone, which was held by the Egyptians, driving them out of the zone and over the border. Nasser was dining with us on that evening in my Counsellor's house, since he did not want to create a precedent by dining in the Embassy. He arrived late, but appeared unworried. The Egyptian radio announced that their Forces had made a successful counter-attack, which in fact had not happened. It was a retaliation on paper, a reasonable expedient. The Israelis remained in the zone.

In December, in retaliation for a series of minor incidents, the Israelis attacked the Syrians on the shores of Lake Tiberias, in contravention of the Armistice, and were condemned by the Security Council. Nasser declared that another attack by the Israelis on the Syrians would lead to action by the Egyptian Forces. Throughout the latter half of the year we and the

Americans were continually pressing the Egyptians to show restraint and to conform to the requirements of the United Nations Truce Supervisory Organisation. Nasser and Dr Mahmoud Fawzi, the Foreign Minister, received our remonstrances without objection, either declaring that they were acting in conformity with the Armistice or promising to conform strictly to its terms if the Israelis would do so too. But tension on the border continued. Both sides retaliated to keep up the morale of their Forces. Both were at fault. The Israelis were more often on top.

In the first months of 1956 the most dangerous issue seemed to be the Israeli threat to dig the Jisr Banat Yacub canal through the Syrian-Israeli demilitarised zone, in order to take Jordan water into the Negev. General Bennike, General Burns's predecessor, had ordered them to stop work on it for a time, though General Burns doubted whether this ruling was justified by the terms of the Armistice Agreement. The Arab view was that it would be aggression and must be met by military action. The Israelis had agreed to defer the work for eighteen months in order to give time to President Eisenhower's special representative, Mr Eric Johnston, to get the agreement of Israelis and Arabs to the scheme for the joint utilisation of the Jordan waters, which would make the Jisr Banat Yacub canal un-necessary. This was very difficult. Mr Johnston brought to his task great patience, ability and tact. He gave me a graphic example of the difficulties with which he had to contend. He was standing on a hill in Jordan with a prominent Jordanian official, looking over a valley which would be irrigated if his scheme came to fruition. He described how the arid valley below them would flow with milk and honey to the benefit of his com-panion's children and grandchildren. The Arab was shaking with emotion. 'And you mean to suggest,' he said, 'that we should co-operate with those people!' The scheme was nicknamed the Johnston plan, which was not the author's fault, but did not help it.

The Egyptians had given Mr Johnston considerable technical help including the loan of Egyptian engineers and, after it had been recast to meet Arab objections, said privately that they favoured the scheme, though they would not stick their necks out by saying so publicly. In the end, the Jordanians and Lebanese were prepared to agree, provided everyone else did. The Iraqis and Saudis remained neutral. The Israelis agreed, though they did not like the amended version. In February 1956 the Arab League met in Cairo to decide the matter. The Syrians refused. No one else was prepared to oppose them and run the risk of being accused of advocating co-operation with the Israelis, which was unavoidable to the extent of sharing with them the use of Lake Tiberias as a storage basin and jointly supervising the distribution of water from it. The Israelis renewed their threats to dig the canal, but were dissuaded by the Americans. People forget how far Nasser was prepared to go at that time in furthering a practical scheme involving Arab-Israeli co-operation.

Throughout the first half of 1955 the Foreign Office and the State Department had been working on the elements of a solution of the three main problems between the Arabs and Israel: refugees, Jerusalem and boundaries. They were prepared to consider lending Israel the money to pay for giving compensation to the refugees for their lost property. But there were intractable difficulties in the way of a solution. The Arabs were inflexible in their view that the refugees must be given the opportunity to return to their homes and that for that purpose the boundaries of Israel must be amended to conform with the United Nations Partition Resolution which would put the old homes of most of them back into an Arab State. The Israelis were not prepared to allow more than relatively few to return.

The only hope seemed to be a compromise whereby some could go back and the rest could be settled in neighbouring Arab States. In the event, there was no settlement. Jerusalem, it was felt, would be permanently partitioned, and so it remained until the Israelis took it all in 1967.

The Israeli acquisition of the Negev in the spring of 1949 was then still a live question in the minds of the Arabs who regarded it as especially outrageous, since it was carried out in direct defiance of the Security Council resolutions of November and December 1948. The Egyptians aimed to secure substantial territorial continuity between Jordan and Egypt, which would mean the cession by Israel to Egypt or Jordan of at least the southern part of the Negev, including the port of Eilat. This would have enabled Nasser to make the Israelis more dependent on the Suez canal and would have made it easier for him to influence Jordan. The Israelis flatly declared that they would not surrender any part of the Negev. It seems curious now that one idea put forward at the time was that a triangle of the Negev on the West should go to Egypt and a triangle on the East to Jordan, the three States of Israel, Egypt and Jordan meeting at a cross-over point to be provided with a bridge or a subway, so that Israeli traffic could pass North and South and Arab traffic East and West. It would not even have survived the caricaturists.

In August 1955 Mr Dulles made a fresh initiative towards a settlement in the form of a general statement looking towards a settlement, but it had no effect. The Western representatives in the Arab States followed it up, but got no positive reaction. But Sir Anthony Eden's speech at the Guildhall in November was received with satisfaction in the Arab States, since he expressed the view that a settlement of the boundaries must take into account the United Nations partition resolution of December 1947 as well as the existing position on the ground. The Arabs had always stuck to the view that this resolution must be carried out, although they had refused to accept it at the time. This was clearly only a bargaining position, since on the 1947 map, although the Arabs were to keep Galilee, the Israelis would have the whole of the Negev; but it was important to the Arabs that for the first time a Western leader acknowledged that the 1947 resolution could not be ignored.

The atmosphere created by this speech seemed at the time to offer some hope of a settlement, in spite of the hostile reaction of the Israelis. Dr Fawzi gave the American ambassador and me his ideas of the terms on which a settlement might be reached. He thought that the refugee question could be settled if finance for compensation were to be forthcoming, provided the Israelis were ready to take back a substantial number of refugees. He did not lay great stress on Jerusalem, which the Egyptians did not seem to regard as the most important issue. Substantial territorial continuity was, he insisted, essential. He claimed the Negev from Beersheba to Eilat, though we judged this to be only a first position. He refused to consider a corridor. He agreed that after a settlement the boycott would be given up and Israeli ships allowed to pass through the canal, though the Arabs would not recognise the State of Israel nor trade nor have any other direct connections with it. Nasser confirmed Dr Fawzi's views, though he was more doubtful whether the refugees' fate could be decided by other people for them. Preliminary views were exchanged, but we did not get very far, though the Americans, with our support, were active in trying to find means of promoting a settlement.

In all the various attempts made at this time to get negotiations started, Nasser was careful not to commit himself, though others sometimes interpreted him in a sense more favourable than he intended. The chances of a settlement were always small. They were soon at vanishing point. The Egyptians were acquiring confidence with their new arms. The Israelis were determined not to give up a yard of the Negev. The refugees were beginning to find that they could bring their influence to bear in the Gaza strip and Jordan and were becoming more politically minded. Iraqi-Egyptian relations were now very bad. Nuri Said had told Mr Macmillan that he would not accuse Nasser of treachery if he moved towards a settlement with Israel. We told Nasser, but he did not trust Nuri. There was no confidence between Arabs.

With increasing tension on the border and the deterioration of relations between Egypt and the West, we could make no direct moves. In June 1956, however, there was once more a gleam of hope for a moment, when it seemed that there might be a slight chance of a serious attempt at a settlement, if we and the Americans could bring in the Soviet Union and India and with them work up to a resolution in the United Nations, perhaps sponsored by some smaller States, but it soon died away. Mr Hammarskjöld was asked to take the matter up on one of his visits to Cairo and agreed with some reluctance, but nothing came of it.

In the spring of 1956 the situation on the border steadily deteriorated. The Egyptians in the Gaza strip were provocative. The Syrian border had not recovered from the Israeli attack on Tiberias. The Jordan border, quiet so long as Glubb commanded the Legion, was now the scene of incidents. The Syrian-Egyptian Joint Command increased tension, though not the effectiveness of the Arab Forces. The Israelis built a kibbutz and fortified their positions in the demilitarised zone of El Auja, against the threat of infiltration by Egyptian Commandos. Mr Hammarskjöld was instructed by the Security Council to try and reduce tension. He extracted declarations from both sides that neither would retaliate against incidents caused by the other and that they would limit themselves to immediate self-defence against attacking forces.

Since Nasser told me in June that the border was only kept quiet by his 'invisible retaliation' and agreed that that meant his commandos, it seems unlikely that he and Mr Hammarskjöld interpreted the right of self-defence in the same way. Mr Hammarskjöld made no progress with the next step, to get both sides to withdraw from positions in which troops were prohibited under Articles 7 and 8 of the Agreement, though the Egyptians were able to agree to this now that they had been pushed out of El Auja and were in any case inclined to move their main border force some distance to the rear, and since they knew that the Israelis would not move anyway. When Mr Hammarskjöld told me that Dr Fawzi had promised to lift the blockade in the Canal as soon as the Israelis conformed to Articles 7 and 8 of the Agreement, I knew that he was misinterpreting what Fawzi had said, and Fawzi confirmed this to me. Both enjoyed subtle and indirect expression and misinterpretations were only too likely between them. Mr Hammarskjöld could only exercise a little moral pressure and was not sanguine that he could improve the situation for more than about three months.

In the event, the incidents began again rather sooner, but stopped after the nationalisation of the Suez Canal Company when the Egyptians were more concerned with other external threats. After the nationalisation of the Canal Company, the Egyptians brought a substantial proportion of their troops back from Sinai to Egypt proper. It was in their interest not to provoke the Israelis. It was in the Israelis' interest not to provoke the Egyptians and thus confuse the issue, now that the Egyptians were in trouble with the West. The calm on the border showed that the Egyptians had been perfectly capable all along of controlling their troops and irregular forces.

One uncertain element in the Egyptian-Israeli situation was the continued existence of the tripartite declaration made by the Americans, British and French in 1950, which asserted the responsibility of the three Powers to prevent changes in boundaries in the Middle East by action within or outside the United Nations. The Egyptians frequently said that they resented it and regarded it as a unilateral declaration which conveyed no right or obligation upon the three Powers, though they were careful not to say that they would not ask for help under the terms of the declaration in the event of an Israeli attack. They were clearly relieved when Mr Selwyn Lloyd told them in Cairo in March 1956, that there would be no question of British Forces entering Egypt by virtue of the declaration without an Egyptian invitation. They said that in their view an open attack by them on the Israelis would bring about an immediate intervention by the Powers on behalf of the Israelis, though they hardly thought that we should relish finding ourselves fighting with the Israelis against the Arabs.

In fact, the declaration, though still having some psychological effect, was a toothless instrument by 1955. The Americans refused to hold staff talks in its context. They would not tell us what part they foresaw for the Sixth Fleet. They stressed the decisive rôle of Congress, but were not prepared to go to Congress for special power for the President in an emergency, as they had during the Far Eastern crisis of 1955 and were again to do after the events of November 1956, to support the so-called Eisenhower doctrine for the Middle East. They implied that action in an emergency would be through and not outside the United Nations. As usual, they were sensitive to the charge that they were ganging up with the Colonial Powers and were clearly unhappy at the prospect of joint action with the British and French in an area in which those Powers had recently held special positions. But they did not formally abrogate the declaration.

Throughout this period we had to assess whether Nasser, having got his arms, would attack Israel in force. He would certainly not have done so before April 1956, when the last British fighting units left the Canal. He told me in the early spring that he was thinking of withdrawing from his advanced positions in Sinai in a month or two when his Forces were used to their new weapons and when the British Forces were no longer in a position to cut his communications. The Egyptian Forces would require many months' training before they were capable of using their new weapons effectively in war, especially the aircraft; but we knew from our experience of Egyptian officers being trained in Britain that they were apt to think that they could master anything without time or effort. We also knew that they were nervous that the Israelis would quickly catch up on any lead that they had got from their Russian arms. However, they would be unlikely to attack the Israelis in a way which would invite intervention by the three Powers under the tripartite declaration and Nasser must have had considerable doubts whether his army could really defeat the Israelis, if only because they would have to fight on the other side of the Sinai desert and their administration was weak.

Nasser cannot have placed any reliance on effective intervention by the other Arab States. Reports that he had decided to attack were never firm enough to be entirely credible. The talk of Communist volunteers was never substantiated. The Russians would have been most unlikely to commit themselves to that extent in 1956, and there was no evidence to support the story, repeated by the Secretary of State in the House of

Commons, that half a million blankets, supposedly for Communist volunteers, had been found in Sinai. We had known long before that the Egyptians had been collecting large stocks of stores in Sinai, presumably because they feared that if there should be a major campaign, the first action of the Israelis would be to destroy the Ferdan bridge over the Canal, the only quick means of supplying the Egyptian army in Sinai. A reliable American journalist, who was in Tel Aviv soon after the events of November 1956, told me that there was no truth in the story of the blankets, which had embarrassed the Israelis. An Egyptian hostile to the régime told me later that Nasser was going to attack Israel in March 1957, but it is unlikely that he had made any such decision, since he was enough of an opportunist not to have any settled intention in advance.

All was quiet on the border from 26 July until towards the end of October, when incidents occurred on the border of Jordan, the Iraqi Forces seemed to be about to enter Jordan on Jordanian invitation and Jordan made a military agreement with Egypt and Syria, directed against Israel. Israel mobilised, but there was no hint in Cairo that the Israelis were about to attack Egypt.

5

By the time I arrived in Egypt, the project to build
a high dam at Aswan had reached an advanced stage.
Its purpose was to provide all-year storage of Nile
water for the irrigation of 1,300,000 acres of desert and
the conversion of 700,000 acres from basin to perennial
irrigation, and electric power. The International Bank
and British consulting engineers had agreed on the
design and the Bank had surveyed the Egyptian
economy. The way was now open for an application to
the Bank for a loan. A consortium of British, German
and French firms had also offered to build the dam and
provide limited credits. There had been some controversy over the right way to develop the use of Nile
waters. It was agreed that both the Blue and White
Niles should be developed. It was considered better to
start with the Blue Nile and leave till later the storage
of water on the White Nile and the drainage of the
Sadd, its great marsh tract. The High Dam would
benefit the Sudan also. It would create a water bank
and would enable the Sudan to draw more water from
the upper reaches of the river. It had to be on Egyptian
territory if the Egyptians were ultimately going to pay
for it. Sudanese agreement would be necessary and
compensation would be paid to them for the relocation

of Wadi Halfa which would be submerged. The Egyptians agreed in principle to meet the small needs of the East African States when they decided what they wanted. As the 'man up river' they were in a strong position. Ethiopia's development schemes were a long way off and they could not reasonably hold up the Egyptian project.

We supported Nasser's view that the High Dam should be the focal point of Egyptian development over the next twenty years. Egypt, with a rapidly expanding population and a dearth of raw materials, needed above all to develop her real wealth, the land. Land reform would help to create a country of peasant proprietors. The dam might just enable the standard of living to keep pace with the growth of the population. It would not solve all Egypt's problems; but it was an imaginative scheme which could help Egypt to become a relatively prosperous and contented country. It was in our interest to help. Our old connection with Egypt had been based on its occupation by British Forces. This was at an end. We had to found our new relationship on a sound, practical basis. A joint effort by the Egyptians and the Western Powers to build the dam would provide this. It would also provide good business for our engineering firms. The Russians were giving arms. This was the best way for us to stay in the picture. In the spring of 1956 the Soviet Ambassador told my Indian colleague that the Soviet Government were not sure whether they wanted to finance the High Dam. It was so large a project in relation to Egyptian resources. It would take so long to build. But he believed that if the West built it, Egypt would remain on their side for the next twenty years.

In November 1955 the Egyptian Finance Minister, Dr Kaissouni and the two engineers responsible for the project, went to London and Washington for talks with the British and American Governments and the International Bank. At about this time it became known that the Russians had said that they were ready to help build the dam; but Nasser did not start negotiations with them while there was a prospect of his getting the dam financed and built by the West. He told tne American Ambassador and me that his priorities for finance were first the Bank, secondly the Western Governments, thirdly the Egyptian Government alone and fourthly the Russians. But he would do it even if he had to go to the Russians. There was a bit of blackmail in this, but Russian statements on their readiness to help were explicit. The British Government took the view that this was a crucial question and that the future Western position in Egypt would be materially affected by the outcome of the High Dam negotiations.

The Egyptian negotiations in Washington were long and involved. The total cost was estimated at $1000 millions, of which $400 millions would be in foreign exchange. It was considered that Egypt would not be able to meet any part of the foreign exchange costs. The Bank agreed to lend $200 millions, provided the British and American Governments would make a grant of the remaining $200 millions. The Bank imposed a number of conditions on the Egyptian Government. They were to take no other foreign loans or substantial suppliers' credits for any purpose during the period of the loan. If they did, the Bank could proportionately reduce its loan. There must be prior agreement with the Sudan. The Bank would have the right to advise on Egyptian economic policy and payment of the loan instalments would be subject to the Bank's being satisfied with the condition of the Egyptian economy and with the progress of the work.

The two Governments also would require the Egyptian Government to observe certain general conditions relating to the management of the Egyptian economy and reserved the right to withhold any portion of the grants in exceptional circumstances. The first stage of the work would require $70 millions in foreign exchange, which would be met solely by the two Governments, the Bank loan being reserved for the second stage. The promise of grants by the two Governments was limited to the first stage. For the later stages they only promised to consider helping to find the foreign exchange required in addition to the Bank loan, which was conditional on the whole foreign exchange being available. The Bank extracted secret letters from the two Governments promising that they would find the foreign exchange required from them in the later stages. The conditions were embodied in a letter of intent from the Bank and in Aides Mémoire from the two Governments. Nasser remained uncommitted.

Nasser objected strongly to what he called the political conditions. He maintained that they amounted to his handing over control of the Egyptian finances to the International Bank, which would, in effect, give the British and American Governments control of his economic and defence policy. He said he was determined not to get into the same mess as Turkey was in through taking American loans. Under this scheme he might be left with the work half finished and no resources to finish it. He must see his way through the financing of the whole project. I argued that the Bank's conditions were standard and had been accepted by other countries and managed to get Nasser to say that, though he would not invite representatives of the Bank to come to Cairo, he would see them if they came.

The President, Mr Eugene Black, responded. Nasser demanded an absolute and irrevocable undertaking from the Bank. Mr Black refused. They compromised on an exchange of letters which satisfied the Egyptian Government that the Bank would not be able to claim excessive rights of inspection of the Egyptian economy and the Bank that they had sufficient right of advice to know what was going on and to intervene if necessary. Mr Black prepared to initial the documents, but there was still one point outstanding. The Egyptians wanted him to delete from the exchange of letters a reference to the Aides Mémoire of the two Governments. I asked Mr Black to find out whether this meant that the Egyptian Government refused to accept the Aides Mémoire. He enquired and confirmed that this was the position. Having dealt with the Bank, the Egyptians would then tackle the two Governments. Mr Black therefore refused to initial the exchange of letters immediately, since the documents from the Bank and the two Governments formed one entity and the Bank's letter was dependent on the Egyptian Government's agreement to the Aides Mémoire also. Mr Black left.

It took me two weeks to get the Egyptian Government's views on the Aides Mémoire. Nasser arranged for Gamal Salem to give them to me. He went through the texts with me orally. I took notes, which he later confirmed subject to one reservation which I incorporated in my notes, giving a copy to the American Ambassador. I thought the Egyptian changes to be generally unobjectionable and in some respects advantageous. They brought the Aides Mémoire into line with the exchange of letters with the Bank. The division of the work into two stages had now been given up, so that the Bank would be involved from the beginning. The Government grants were to be made not directly to the Egyptian Government but to the Bank, which would enable us to negotiate conditions with the Bank rather than with the Egyptian Government. We should not of course agree to the proposal that we should pay the Bank our contributions at once, so that they could earn interest. That was only a try-on.

After what seemed to us to be an unconscionable time, the British Government agreed to our views, though not to making their grant through the Bank, and authorised the Embassy in Washington to start negotiations with the State Department, which however made no move. The negotiations stuck. The Americans were reappraising their policy towards Egypt. Egyptian co-operation with the Communist Governments was increasing and the Americans were clearly going to find it difficult to make a grant for the dam. Moreover, there was some doubt whether the Egyptians had not already undermined the economic basis of the project, which even with the loan and grants would stretch their resources. Their Defence Budget for 1956-7 showed an increase of £E22.5 million, making an allocation for defence of £E75.4 million out of a total estimated revenue of £E280.5 million. Russian statements suggested that there would be Russian loans for industrial development. Rumours that the Russians would finance the dam increased and it was suggested that arrangements for this would be made during Nasser's visit to the Soviet Union in the autumn.

The American Ambassador and I urged on Washington and London that the offer should be maintained. The first critical issue of this period between us and the Egyptians had been the conditions for the purchase of American arms in 1955. This was the second. Whatever we thought of Nasser's recent behaviour, however dim the prospects of reasonable relations with him, we believed that the West must finance the dam if there were to be any prospect of co-operation over a long period with the new Egypt, whoever became its leader. The preparatory work for the dam was such that it would be some years before we had to pay anything and by that time Egypt's political path would be clear. Our position would be safeguarded through our arrangements with the Bank and the Bank's arrangements with the Egyptian Government. We should clinch the matter

before Nasser went to Moscow. But if the two Governments decided not to go on with the proposal, they
should not withdraw the offers themselves, but should
put the onus on Nasser to refuse the terms offered him.

In the middle of June Mr Eugene Black passed
through Cairo and saw Nasser who gave him the impression that he still wanted the dam to be built by the
West and made no mention of the Russian offer. In
the first half of July Nasser saw Ahmed Hussain, the
Egyptian Ambassador in Washington, at Bourg el Arab.
Ahmed Hussain had urged me a few days previously to
get London to finish the negotiations without further
delay and made no secret of the importance which he
attached to this. We heard later that at this interview
Nasser had told him that he had already given up hope
of the money for the dam coming from the West and that
when this was confirmed, he would, in retaliation,
nationalise the Suez Canal Company. Ahmed Hussain
protested. Nasser replied: 'Keep your nerve and it will
be all right.' Ahmed Hussain begged to be allowed to
try and finish the negotiations in Washington. Nasser
agreed. Ahmed Hussain went back to Cairo and asked
for the text of the Egyptian objections to the Aides
Mémoire. Gamal Salem had left the Government. My
letters to him recording the objections could not be
found. He took a copy from the American Ambassador
and flew to Washington.

By this time the two Governments had decided that
they would go back on their offers, but not how they
would do it. The British advocated caution. Ahmed
Hussain announced immediately after his arrival in
Washington that Egypt was ready to accept the
American and British offers. This forced Mr Dulles's
hand. He told the British Ambassador that he was
preoccupied by the effect of this matter on the relations
between Congress and the Administration. The Foreign
Aid Bill was due to come before the House of

Representatives in a few days' time. There was strong opposition to aid for Egypt. The House was likely to use this question to challenge the Bill and to dictate policy to the State Department by adding a rider prohibiting aid to Egypt. The Administration did not want to give Congress this opportunity. He would therefore have to announce the withdrawal of the offer without further delay. On 19 July he announced that the offer was withdrawn owing to the economic condition of Egypt. The British Government quickly followed suit.

On that evening Nasser was due to return to Cairo from Brioni with Nehru. He arrived at 2 a.m. I waited to meet him, since there was a Commonwealth Prime Minister with him and since both my American and Soviet colleagues were determined to be there, at whatever hour he arrived. At 1 a.m. a foreign correspondent telephoned to me the news of the withdrawal of the American offer. I told Dr Kaissouni, who gave a startled gasp and said nothing. A day later he complained bitterly of the reflection on the country's economy in the statements of the two Governments. On the morning of 19 July I went to the airport to see Nehru off. Nasser was very glum. I spoke about the High Dam to Colonel Zachariya Mohieddin, the Minister of the Interior. He replied: 'It is not so much the withdrawal of the money which we mind. We can find other ways of financing the High Dam. It is the way in which it was done.' This action seemed for the moment to have convinced Nasser that the Americans had turned against him. A few days later, he turned on them in a bitter, savage attack in his speech at the opening of the Suez-Cairo pipe-line, accusing them of perfidy, a speech which elicited a strong official protest from the American Government. But the real retaliation was to come. On 26 July Nasser announced the nationalisation of the Suez Canal Company.

6

IN December 1954 the Arab League Foreign
Ministers met in Cairo and were reported to have
agreed informally that Arab security should be founded
on the Arab League Security Pact and that no Arab
State should adhere to Western military pacts, though
there is some doubt how far the Iraqi Foreign Minister
was speaking with the authority of the Iraqi Government. Nasser claimed to have received a shock when the
Baghdad Pact was arranged in January 1955. He professed to regard the Pact as a conspiracy between
Britain and Iraq and as a betrayal of him by Nuri Said.
Nuri claimed to have told him about it in advance.
Whatever the truth, Nasser immediately started violent
propaganda against Iraq and the Pact, and the battle of
words continued for some weeks until the Egyptians
saw that they were achieving nothing by it and allowed
it to die down.

In the spring, my predecessor, Sir Ralph Stevenson,
on instructions from London, assured Nasser that no
attempt would be made to secure the adherence to
the Pact of other Arab States. Nasser told him that he
would not regard it as action hostile to Egyptian interests
that non-Arab States, such as Britain, should join the
initial members, Iraq and Turkey, as members of the
Pact. There was a lull until the autumn. In October the

British Government tried to secure the adherence of Jordan to the Pact. I gave my opinion that this was unwise in view of the Egyptian reactions to be expected. I was told that we could not change our policy just because Nasser objected. I replied that what I objected to was that the policy had been changed. The Jordanian Government had asked for more arms. Some fighter aircraft were sent as a gift and General Templer was sent to Amman in order to discuss Jordan's request and to encourage Jordan to join the Pact. He failed and the Jordanian Government fell.

I was instructed to say that General Templer's mission had not been to press Jordan to join the Pact. He had visited Jordan at the request of the Jordanian Government to discuss the supply of arms, and the question of the Pact had naturally come into the discussion. According to General Templer's account, he had told the Jordanian Government that it was time for them to make up their minds on the Pact and that the supply of arms would depend on their attitude to it. He attributed his failure to the pusillanimity of the Jordanian Prime Minister, Egyptian propaganda and Saudi money, all features of the Jordanian landscape at that moment of which Ministers at home were fully aware. General Templer bears no blame for the failure of his mission. His instructions were misconceived. A more cautious approach through the Ambassador would have had a better chance of success. When I subsequently read General Templer's straightforward account, I could only conclude that what I had been told to tell Nasser about it was not a fair statement of the purpose of the mission. But that was all over. Nasser reacted as expected. He knew from his own intelligence sources in Jordan exactly what had happened. Egyptian propaganda was turned on at full blast; large amounts of Saudi money changed hands and Anglo-Egyptian relations received a new jolt.

I protested to Nasser. He did not deny that he had acted against what he believed to be the purpose of the Templer Mission. His position on the Pact was based on his concept of a defence alliance among Arab States, springing from an Arab initiative, obviously his own. Before he took Russian arms, he used to say that the Arab alliance would give facilities to the Western Powers for defence against Communist attack; but they would not make a formal alliance with the West. Such an alliance would entail the risk of a revival of Western influence in Egypt and elsewhere in the Arab world. It would clash with his basic position that Egypt must be and must appear to be completely independent. He maintained this position throughout. From this time he argued that the British Government, with the help of Nuri Said, were pursuing a policy of hostility to Egypt. They were trying to isolate Egypt, to encircle it with a ring of new Arab members of the Baghdad Pact, Jordan, then Lebanon, Syria, Saudi Arabia, the Sudan and Libya, in order to put pressure on Egypt and reduce it again to dependence on the British. He had no long-term policy. He only reacted in his own defence. There was a chain of action and counter-action. Where would it lead? What was our long-term policy? If only he knew that, he would know where he stood. I argued back that his theory that we were engaged in a plot to isolate him was nonsense, that he had nothing to fear from the Pact which was directed against the Communists and not against him and that his motives were equally suspect in Britain. It was not true that he never acted, but only reacted. He often acted against our interests and we had to defend ourselves against him. Neither of us shifted our ground.

Mr Selwyn Lloyd, the new Foreign Secretary, called a conference of British representatives in the Middle East for the first week of January 1956. On 1 January I saw Nasser before leaving for London. I told him that I

hoped it was a good augury that I should be his first
visitor in the New Year. It certainly did not work out
like that. I wanted to find some way of breaking the
vicious circle of action and counter-action, as Nasser
called it, and of getting away from the repetition of
sterile argument. The only way of doing this was to
come to some sort of understanding on the Baghdad
Pact which would induce Nasser to accept its existence
and stop hostile action and propaganda against it. In
this conversation the outlines of a possible deal began
to emerge. If the members of the Pact agreed that there
should be no more Arab members, Nasser might be
brought to accept the Pact. If he wished, he could at
the same time try and revivify the Arab League
Security Pact, as the basis of Arab defence. Iraq, I
argued, had every reason to be a member of the
Pact by virtue of its exposed position. It looked both
ways. It was a frontier State (or as near as made no
difference) and an Arab State. It could be a member of
both the Baghdad Pact and the Arab Security Pact and
could be the link between the two. At this stage I could
not commit myself to more than an examination of
something along these lines. Nasser neither accepted
nor rejected the idea. It was always possible that all he
wanted was that we should stop trying to get Jordan
into the Pact, so that he might have time to build up an
opposition circle of pro-Egyptian States. But some
arrangement on these lines seemed to offer the only
chance of stopping the deterioration of our relations
and giving us a period of quiet during which we could
explore ways of stabilising the situation.

In London, not surprisingly, the emphasis was on
strengthening the Pact, supporting our friends and
cherishing our relations with the oil-producing States.
However, an official in the Foreign Office said to me
that he had started his job with the belief that the key
to the Middle East was Egypt, and that we could not

hope to see a Middle East favourable to our interests if we ignored Egypt. We were tempted by suddenly finding a concrete, positive policy, the Baghdad Pact. It seemed a success and we pushed ahead with it. But he now realised that his original view had been correct. I suggested a visit by the Secretary of State, taking up a promise made by Mr Macmillan a short time before, in the hope that he might reach an understanding with Nasser.

I returned to Cairo. Within a day or two, trouble in Jordan began again. Rioting broke out among the refugees and the town mobs, incited by Egyptian and Saudi propaganda. I was instructed to go for Nasser for his part in inflaming the situation. He did not take the trouble to deny that he had had a hand in the matter. He justified it as purely defensive action designed to prevent attempts to bring Jordan into the Baghdad Pact and to isolate Egypt. He said that the situation had not been created by Egypt and Saudi Arabia. It was caused by genuine public feeling in Jordan. He had a list of all the people who were being paid by the Saudis in Jordan. They were all people without influence. Here again was action and counter-action. What was our policy? Where would it lead? We had our usual argument and got nowhere.

For some time Nasser had been trying to build up an Arab group opposed to the Baghdad Pact. In October 1955 he had made bilateral pacts with Syria and Saudi Arabia. The three countries now offered Jordan a subsidy, 'in case Jordan should no longer receive a subsidy from the British Government', as they put it. I protested to Nasser that this seemed to be an attempt to disturb the Anglo-Jordanian Treaty, in spite of his previous protestations to me that he had nothing against it. He replied that he had been told by a member of the Jordanian Government at the time of the Templer Mission that General Templer had threatened that the subsidy would be withdrawn if Jordan did not join the Pact. The alternative offer had only been made in case this threat were put into effect. He had been quite happy about our relations with Jordan. Why had we not been content with that? It was like a man with a gold watch in his left-hand waistcoat pocket. The watch is there and no one thinks anything of it. But he takes it out of his pocket, flashes it in the public view and wants to transfer it to his right-hand waistcoat pocket. He runs the risk of having it stolen on the way. I denied his story about General Templer immediately and again after reference to London; but Nasser did not believe me. I kept up the pressure on the subsidy question with both Nasser and Dr Fawzi, making it clear that there was little chance of our affairs taking a turn for the better so long as the offer remained. Dr Fawzi never promised to withdraw it formally, but said more than once that, provided there were no new shocks, it could be allowed quietly to lapse.

The situation in Jordan became quiet, but remained uneasy. The Foreign Secretary decided to visit Cairo at the beginning of March on his way to a SEATO meeting in Karachi. On the way back, he was to visit Teheran, Baghdad and Ankara. Here was a chance of arriving at a truce with Nasser. The auspices were not good. From the time of the Templer Mission anti-British propaganda had again started on Cairo radio, through the 'Voice of the Arabs' directed to the Arab world, which concentrated on the Baghdad Pact, and the East African programmes which dealt mostly with local issues. Dr Fawzi appeared to be anxious about the situation and keen on bringing off something during the Foreign Secretary's visit. We went repeatedly over the ground, trying to work out the basis for a political truce. From Nasser's statements it seemed that he was now thinking on the lines sketched out in our conversation of 1 January, the co-existence of the alliance of frontier States against the Russian threat and the Arab defensive system. We were not concerned by Nasser's plans for joint Arab defence. They were unlikely to get beyond propaganda. Nasser would probably continue to try and get Iraq out of the Baghdad Pact, as Fawzi virtually admitted. A political truce which required him to stop his radio attacks would make it more difficult for him to succeed. We had nothing to lose by trying this line. The argument for pressing Arab States to become members of the Baghdad Pact had been that the momentum must be maintained, that a struggle for influence was being waged between Egypt and Iraq and that once the initiative was lost, Iraqi influence would be lost and Egypt would come out on top. But that was no longer a practical policy since Egypt had succeeded in swinging Jordan away from the Pact. There was now no chance of new Arab members. The arguments were in favour of trying for a truce which would, at least for a time, arrest the slide into hostility between us and give a chance for things to settle down.

It was widely believed that Nasser's personal agents in the Egyptian Embassies abroad were the military attachés, who sometimes allowed their enthusiasm to outrun their discretion. A senior civilian official of the Ministry of Foreign Affairs told one of my colleagues in 1957 after we had left, that after his experiences in the last two years he realised that he would be wise to serve as Ambassador only in a post where there was no military attaché. In January the Iraqis announced the arrest of a servant of the Egyptian Military Attaché's office in Baghdad and demanded the Attaché's recall. The charges were of attempts at subversion and bomb plots. During the trial Nasser loosed off his most vitriolic propaganda against the Iraqis and Iraqi-Egyptian relations reached a dangerously low point. Nuri asked me to intervene with Nasser. Neither did he trust his Ambassador in Cairo, a legacy of old Iraqi family history. Having spoken to the Iraqi Ambassador, I told Nasser that Nuri wanted a request from Nasser to him to withdraw the case in the Iraqi Courts against the Egyptian accused in the interests of inter-Arab relations. Nasser would not do anything which would amount to an admission of complicity and replied that Nuri should withdraw the charge on his own initiative. Nuri refused. The accused man was convicted and sent back to Egypt, and retired into an obscure position in Nasser's private office. Nuri won the round on points. We could not expect much improvement in our relations so long as Iraqi-Egyptian relations were bad. We were too closely involved in Iraq. Iraqi-Egyptian relations were not likely to improve so long as Nuri and Nasser were still in position.

As March wore on, the atmosphere grew worse. I was instructed to protest against an attack by the Egyptian radio on General Glubb. Nasser said that he had given no instructions to attack Glubb and that if he did, I should notice the difference. He complained to me about Glubb's political activity in Jordan and produced secret reports from his agents in the Arab Legion, giving accounts of Glubb's alleged propaganda in the Legion in favour of Jordan's joining the Baghdad Pact. He told me that he had photocopies of Glubb's letters to the Jordanian Minister of Defence, one of which complained about the distribution of Nasser's picture by the Egyptian Embassy. He said that these demonstrated Glubb's political activities outside his proper responsibilities. A few days later, only ten days before the Foreign Secretary's visit, the Egyptian radio delivered a series of full-scale attacks on Glubb. There was no doubt when Nasser turned the tap full on. I protested strongly to Dr Fawzi, saying that this was a thoroughly bad augury for the Foreign Secretary's visit.

Mr Selwyn Lloyd arrived on 29 February. On that evening there was a dinner party with Nasser at the

Tahera Palace. During dinner, I was called out by one of the Embassy staff, who handed me a telegram containing the news that King Hussain had dismissed General Glubb. I put the telegram into my pocket and said nothing. After dinner, there was general political conversation. Nasser was handed a slip of paper. This, I thought, might be the same news. I passed a note to Sir Harold Caccia who was sitting next to Mr Selwyn Lloyd. He did not pass it on until after the meeting. Some time later I discussed this incident with Nasser. He said he remembered my passing the note, that at the moment Dr Fawzi was talking about the tripartite declaration and that he had wondered what comment I could have on that subject. It was an example of the conspirator's memory for detail. I managed to head the conversation off Jordanian affairs. On the way back to the Embassy, I told Mr Selwyn Lloyd the news. He was greatly upset. He was convinced that Nasser had known of General Glubb's dismissal and half convinced that Nasser had planned it to coincide with his visit. It put him in a most embarrassing situation. He was being attacked in the British Press for coming to Cairo at all. This would be interpreted as a deliberate affront which he had to swallow. He toyed with the idea of refusing to go to the meeting with Nasser which had been arranged for the morning, but rightly decided to keep the engagement.

The meeting was polite but not cordial. The conversation was on familiar ground and Mr Selwyn Lloyd repeated all the complaints which I had made continually to Nasser and Dr Fawzi. The proposition emerged that there should be no new Arab members of the Baghdad Pact, that Nasser would acquiesce in Iraqi membership of it and stop anti-British and anti-Pact propaganda and that he would at the same time try and revive the Arab League Security Pact with Iraq as a member of it also. Mr Selwyn Lloyd did not reject the proposal as contrary either to the wording of the Baghdad Pact or to British policy. He said that he would consult the other members of the Pact when he visited their capitals on his return journey from Karachi, and his colleagues when he returned home on 16 March. He would then send an answer to Nasser's proposal.

In the car on the way to the airport, Mr Selwyn Lloyd, Sir Harold Caccia and I discussed the situation. I suggested that we had the choice of two unpalatable courses. We could make a bargain such as Nasser had proposed. We could not expect genuine co-operation from him in return for it. We should have to look out for Egyptian attempts to injure our interests elsewhere in the Arab world, but we might be able to take the edge off Nasser's hostility and arrive at a modus vivendi of a sort. The alternative was to adopt a thoroughly tough policy against him. We must then expect unrelieved hostility from him. We knew that he had the power to hurt our interests. If we decided on this course, we must hit hard and accept all the serious international consequences which would follow. I recommended that we should try the first course. I was supported by Sir Harold Caccia, who said that it was at least questionable whether we had now got the power to carry through a tough forward policy.

Nasser always maintained that he did not know of General Glubb's dismissal at the time of our dinner party. That is probably true. Our communications were quick. That does not imply that he was not aware that something was going on. Many people had had an inkling of it. A British correspondent had come back from Jordan the week before and had told me that Glubb would not last three months. A *Times* correspondent in Amman reported later that it had been a local coup engineered by the King and the young Lt.-Col., Ali Abu Nawar. I referred to this in a conversation with Nasser and added that his violent propaganda against General Glubb only a few days before Mr Selwyn Lloyd's visit had naturally made many people think that he had engineered the plot. He replied petulantly that he had told me at the time that his propaganda was only his defence against General Glubb's political activities against him. It was not the prelude to a plot for Glubb's dismissal. He asked whether we had really not known ourselves what was happening. I believed at the time that Nasser knew that Glubb was on the way out, that his propaganda was intended to help this on, that his military attaché was almost certainly encouraging Ali Abu Nawar to get rid of Glubb, that Nasser may have known what Ali Abu Nawar was up to, but that he did not then know that the king had been persuaded and was at that moment dismissing Glubb.

The Foreign Secretary arrived in Bahrain and was greeted by a pro-Nasser anti-British riot. It had its origin in local political agitation stirred up by Egyptian intrigues. It happened by chance at that moment because a crowd was returning from a football match. Whatever its origin, it had its effect. To the British Press and some members of the House of Commons it was another deliberate Nasser plot against Mr Selwyn Lloyd. This was followed after two or three days by a meeting in Cairo of Nasser, King Saud and President Shukri Kuwatli of Syria, at which the three Heads of State formally renewed their promise to King Hussain to pay the Jordan subsidy if the British withdrew it, and tried without success to get him to join them in Cairo. I immediately took this up with Dr Fawzi. I asked him how we could believe Nasser's statement that he was not acting against British interests when he chose this moment to renew the Egyptian promise of a subsidy to Jordan in terms which clearly encouraged King Hussain to renounce the British subsidy and the British alliance. Dr Fawzi was not convincing. He replied that they had to do it because the Jordanian Government had denied that they had been offered a subsidy. The three Governments had to prove their good faith. Now the offer could be allowed to die quietly, provided there was no fresh move in Jordan from the other side.

The atmosphere now began to thicken. Nasser told an American correspondent in an interview for publication that he did not believe Mr Selwyn Lloyd's statement to him that the British Government were not trying to influence the Sudanese Government against Egypt. A few days after Mr Selwyn Lloyd left, propaganda attacks on the British started again on both the foreign radio services. I asked Nasser how he could expect co-operation between us if this happened as soon as Mr Selwyn Lloyd's back was turned. Nasser replied that he had given no instructions to the radio officials to attack the British. He could assure me that the extracts about which I complained had not been broadcast on the Voice of the Arabs, which he followed very closely. He would enquire about the complaints against the African Service.

This incident got me into some difficulty. When the war of words became hotter, the extracts which I had shown to Nasser were publicly declared to be British forgeries. One was a forgery. I had been instructed to protest about four extracts taken from the reliable BBC monitoring service. I had added for good measure one which had been reported by the Political Resident in the Gulf and which proved to be a highly coloured version of the original, and one which had been given me by the American Embassy and which proved to have been made up by an Egyptian employed by them to monitor Egyptian broadcasts. By the time this came out, it was no longer of any importance. The affair was drowned in the flood of abuse which was by that time

being broadcast in Cairo and which would have
provided material for many protests.

On the British side too, things were not made easier.
When Mr Selwyn Lloyd left Cairo airport, he wisely
said that the question of General Glubb's dismissal was
a matter for the Jordanian Government which
employed him, but that General Glubb had been a
good and loyal friend of the Arabs. But in England
the reaction was very different. General Glubb was
treated as if he had been an official of the British
Government. His dismissal was treated in the Press and
in Parliament as a resounding British diplomatic defeat
at the hands of Nasser. This was excellent propaganda
for Nasser and disposed of the useful story then circulat-
ing in the Arab world that Glubb had really been dismissed through a British intrigue. On 7 March the
Prime Minister said in the House of Commons: 'I want
to say something on the subject of Egypt. For some time
past, we know, the Egyptian broadcasts have kept up a
stream of abuse against Glubb Pasha, and that has been
distributed all over Jordan. To try to disrupt a treaty
between Jordan and ourselves is utterly inconsistent
with assurances of friendly relations. If the Egyptians
generally want friendly relations with the Western
Powers, they can be obtained, but not at any price. One
way of ensuring that Egypt does not get them is to
pursue a policy which, on the one hand, professes
friendship and, on the other, incites hostility.' He had
every justification, though it would perhaps have been
better not to imply that Nasser had been powerful
enough to secure General Glubb's dismissal.

Mr Selwyn Lloyd returned to London and I awaited
his promised reply to Nasser. According to Nasser's
subsequent account, when by 25 March no reply had
been received, he tried the method which he had used
during the negotiations leading to the Base Agreement.
He gave interviews for publication to the *Sunday*

Times and the *Observer*. He said that he had intended that these should show him in conciliatory mood and help towards agreement on the lines which he had proposed. In these interviews he put forward his thesis that the efforts to get more Arab members into the Baghdad Pact were an attempt to isolate Egypt and that an understanding should be reached that there should be no more Arab members. I must confess that in Cairo we saw little in these articles of special note.

The British Government did not take that view. On that Sunday an official statement was issued in the name of the Foreign Office spokesman that Nasser's deeds did not match his words, that he professed co-operation but was really out to destroy British interests and that an agreement by the members of the Pact not to have new Arab members was impossible, since it was open to any State to join the Pact in the exercise of its sovereign prerogatives. We did not however intend to press any State to join. This interpretation of the Baghdad Treaty was arguable. The Treaty provided that any member of the Arab League or other State having an interest in the area could join, but this did not prevent the members of the Pact from refusing a request for membership. Nasser had made his proposal to the Foreign Secretary, who had not argued that it was inconsistent with the Treaty, but had promised to consider it. On the other hand, by making a public statement, Nasser had invited a public reply and his conduct since Mr Selwyn Lloyd's visit had made the atmosphere worse. Nasser took this statement as a declaration of war. He told the Egyptian Press and Radio to attack the British with all possible force. The manoeuvres over the Baghdad Pact were the main cause of the real deterioration in Anglo-Egyptian relations which now set in. We were on the road to open hostility.

7

THE time for protests was past. The Egyptian Press
and Radio poured out unrestrained abuse. The British
Press whipped up a campaign against Nasser in reply.
He was public enemy No. 1. Why had we any truck
with him? We should use the old gun-boat policy and
make him give in. All this built up Nasser's status as
an Arab leader. In April, Egypt, Saudi Arabia and the
Yemen made a military agreement on the lines of the
existing agreements between Egypt and Syria and Egypt
and Saudi Arabia. It should have been treated with
contempt. *The Times* and other newspapers declared it
to be another blow aimed by Egypt at the British
position in Aden and a diplomatic defeat for Britain.
The Egyptian Press was delighted by this reaction and
proclaimed a victory for Nasser.

At the end of March a new message had reached me
from London for communication to Nasser. It ignored
the fact that I was still awaiting the message which the
Foreign Secretary had promised to send to Nasser on
his return to London. At my suggestion it was redrafted
in the form of the promised reply, with reasons for the
refusal of Nasser's proposal. It gave Nasser's statement
to the Press as the reason and again stated that we were
not pressing any Arab State to join the Pact. For the

first time since the Sudan affair, I failed to see Nasser. I gave the message to Dr Fawzi. I had no contact with Nasser throughout April and the first half of May.

Cairo was the headquarters of dissident movements throughout the Middle East and North Africa. Among others, the Algerian rebels had an office there. Egypt was sending arms and funds to Algeria and was training Algerian guerrillas. In late 1955 the French had stopped deliveries of arms under their current contracts with Egypt, as a result of Egyptian anti-French propaganda. In the early spring deliveries were resumed on the understanding that anti-French propaganda would be called off. The French Minister for External Affairs, Monsieur Pineau, visited Cairo in March and, to our surprise, put his name to a joint communiqué with Nasser, who admitted having sent arms and trained guerrillas, but claimed that he had stopped the training. This was, I believe, true. But he was still supplying arms. He offered to bring an Algerian delegation to Cairo to talk to the French, but the proposal leaked in France and nothing came of it.

Relations with the French were slipping; but the real abuse was reserved for the British. In the meanwhile, Nasser continued to act against British interests in other parts of the Arab world. He had told me that the accusations about his activities against the British in Aden and Bahrain were groundless, since he had no organisation in either place. I judged that the reply was an evasion. Representatives of extremist parties in both were received in Cairo and we believed that they were given material support. The Voice of the Arabs did all it could to disturb affairs wherever the British still had a special position in the Arab world. Only on the Buraimi issue was Egyptian propaganda half-hearted. Nasser had told me that it was not of real interest to Egypt and that he had only sent a public message in support of the Saudi claim at King Saud's special request. We heard that some of the arms sent westwards through Libya were hidden in Libya for use in a future pro-Egyptian coup. In the Sudan, efforts were concentrated on strengthening pro-Egyptian factions and trying to win over the leaders of the sects to Egyptian interests.

The British Government now seemed convinced that Nasser was our enemy. Officials were asked to produce ideas how we could oppose his aims. They produced a paper which seemed to us to consist of what Joe Allsop, the American columnist who had recently been in London with his ear close to the ground, described as 'contraptions'. We commented that the ideas in the paper were pinpricks which would increase Nasser's hostility to us and improve his position in the Arab world. We should not fall between two stools. We could adopt a really tough policy against increasing pressure from world opinion, or we could be cautious, keep our relations with Egypt at a low level, and try and avoid violent hostility on either side.

The Americans were also re-thinking their policy towards Nasser and we heard that Washington saw no further hope of co-operating with him and regarded him as practically sold to the Communists. He was by now certainly hostile to us, though we still did not believe that he would allow himself to come wholly under Communist control. We heard that Ministers were thinking of stopping or at least slowing down evacuation. This seemed to us to be most dangerous. We had an agreement and had no valid reason for not carrying it out. Our action would be immediately observable to the Egyptians, who would retaliate by again unleashing their Commandos on British troops, and we should be back to the worst days of the troubles before the 1954 Agreement, without any reasonable excuse. The Egyptians could make life impossible for the contractors. In any case, it was too late. Many troops had already left and the remainder were not in a position to defend themselves against hostile action. We protested. I was told that my letter had been timely. Ministers had been considering the idea. We were able to reinforce the unanimous civil and military advice against tampering with the execution of the Agreement.

In May Dr Fawzi took a hand again, being apparently increasingly disturbed at the turn of events. The Baghdad Pact issue seemed now to be much less important. After some long conversations with me, Dr Fawzi told the Iraqi Ambassador and me that if we asked for interviews with Nasser, he would see us. I took the opportunity. I argued to Dr Fawzi and to Nasser that it was ridiculous that our public relations should be so bad. For the first time in modern history there was no specifically Anglo-Egyptian dispute. The Sudan and the Base were out of the way. The Base Agreement was being carried out harmoniously. We had offered to help finance the most important Egyptian development project and only the details remained to be negotiated. We regretted that they had bought Russian arms, but we recognised their right to buy arms where they liked. We deplored the continuance of the Arab-Israeli dispute, but that was not a specifically Anglo-Egyptian issue and we still looked to Egypt to take the lead in settling it. Our quarrels were all on matters outside Egypt. What good did it do to Egypt to interfere in the constitutional reforms in Zanzibar? Why should Anglo-Egyptian relations be disturbed by violent Egyptian attacks on the British position in Aden? I repeated that it was all very well for Nasser to say that he only reacted and never acted. That was not true. He often acted against us and we reacted.

I asked why Nasser could not follow the example of Mustapha Kemal. I had heard that he had read the biography of Mustapha Kemal, *Grey Wolf*, seven times.

Had he not realised that Mustapha Kemal was successful because he had convinced the Powers that he was not interested in foreign adventures, but only in the development of his own country? Why could we not have a period of quiet on both sides? The British had an excellent record in dealing with territories dependent on them. They were responsive to political developments and had succeeded in adjusting their relations with many countries in Asia and Africa. What they had done elsewhere, they could do also in the Arab world, given time and peace. But Nasser was being hostile to us throughout the Arab world and Africa. Why had he attacked our position in Jordan just after Mr Selwyn Lloyd had left, by formally offering a subsidy in place of our subsidy? Why did he publicly state that he did not believe what Mr Selwyn Lloyd had told him about the Sudan? Why did he order such virulent propaganda to be put out against us? How could he hope for good relations with us if he acted like this? He accused us of being insensitive to Arab opinion. But we had a public opinion too and he was grossly insensitive to it. And what was the practical point at issue over the Baghdad Pact? We had said that we should not press any country to join it. Nasser knew that no Arab country was now likely to join it. He could afford to let the Pact be. We now had an opportunity to restore the situation. We were approaching the end of the evacuation of the British troops from Egypt. This could be made the occasion for the kind of rhetoric which would only make matters worse. But it could also be used to make a new start. Nasser had been used to say that he could not co-operate until the last soldier had left Egypt. This moment was coming. Could he not make a gesture of friendship at that time? Could we not gradually get onto better terms again? This was perhaps a crucial moment when our affairs would either be restored or plunge into worse disorder from which both Britain and Egypt would suffer.

Nasser apologised for not having seen me. He said that it was nothing personal. He had felt that he could not be frank with me. He could not be frank even now. He had been accused by the British Government of trickery and treachery, an accusation for which there were no grounds whatever. He had made a proposal to Mr Selwyn Lloyd. The reply was a public attack on him in an official statement. It was only when he was convinced that the British Government were hostile to him and when the British Press started their violent attacks on him that he had reacted by directing his Press and Radio to attack back. It was, as he had always said, a chain of action and reaction. Where would it end? He would consider whether he could make a friendly gesture when the last soldier had left, though he feared that it would be met by hostility. We were at it for three hours. At least we knew where we stood.

We now had to get over the awkward period of the final evacuation without further damage to our interests and to try and deflect the course of events into a more favourable channel. The Foreign Secretary went a long way to help. I was authorised to say that any friendly statement would be met by the like, and the Foreign Secretary gave a friendly message to the London correspondent of an Egyptian newspaper. Nasser hinted that he would like Mr Nutting, the Minister of State who had signed the 1954 Base Agreement, to come to the celebrations as the British Government's representative. I reported this to London. It was a difficult decision for them.

When after three days no answer had come, Nasser invited General Sir Brian Robertson as his private guest, and told me that he had done so. I advised that Sir Brian should come. He accepted the invitation as a public duty. The last British soldier slipped away unobtrusively on 15 June. There was no ceremony of withdrawal. I had hoped that the last troops would leave before the end of May, which would have made the Egyptian celebrations something of an anti-climax, but the planners would not be hurried. As it was, even the anticipation of the final date by three days was characterised by the Egyptian Press as another British trick. Up to the day before the start of the celebrations I was urging Dr Fawzi to keep off anti-British demonstrations, which would be splashed across the London headlines. Dr Fawzi in his usual oblique way made it clear enough that he either could not or would not stop the young revolutionaries giving vent to their feelings. It was not surprising. The country had been occupied since 1882 and was for the first time in modern history wholly master of itself. It was to be expected that the occasion would be represented as the birth of freedom from a tyrannical foreign occupier.

I did what I could with Nasser and Fawzi, but viewed the whole affair with some apprehension, as I observed the cartoons of Denshawai, the Egyptian emotional equivalent to Amritsar, the colossal cardboard commando bestriding a street in the main square, and the mounting excitement. Sir Brian Robertson arrived. He was understandably wary. He had an important position in British public life. He did not want to find himself pilloried in the British Press for taking part in anti-British ceremonies. The Foreign Office was also nervous and woke me up in the middle of the night with a most immediate telegram saying that the *Daily Mail* had reported an objectionable passage from Nasser's speech at Port Said. Did Sir Brian and I think that he should return home? The passage was taken out of its context, a historical review. It was not too bad. We calmed them down and the General stayed.

We did not attend Nasser's main speech. In it he made what might be construed as a friendly reference to Britain, but declared as his aim the liberation of the Arabs from Morocco to Baghdad. I asked Dr Fawzi if that meant that Nasser would try and overturn all British alliances and treaties in the Middle East. Dr Fawzi neatly replied that it would only apply to Britain if I regarded any of the Arab States as being under British domination. Nasser also gave a friendly message addressed to Britain to the correspondent of the *News Chronicle* in reply to the Foreign Secretary's message to an Egyptian correspondent. I wrote to him that I was glad to see it and that I hoped we should move towards better times. He replied in the words of the preamble of the 1954 Agreement that he hoped we were approaching a new era of friendship between our peoples. I have always been sorry that I failed to rescue that document from the holocaust of my records in November. The parade passed off without incident and we were happy to see that the Centurions performed better than the Russian tanks. The procession of floats was obviously going to be more or less offensive to us and we did not attend it. The symbol of the Revolution was erected at the end of the Kasr ul Nil bridge, a huge eagle apparently made out of kerosene oil tins and decorated in neon lights with a symbol resembling a soda water syphon crossed with a bottle opener. Cairo returned to normal.

Propaganda now died down and we allowed ourselves a little hope. An official Trade Mission headed by the Minister of Commerce and the Head of the Bank Misr left for London. Nationalist influences were making difficulties for foreign firms and trying to push the foreigner out, but the Finance Minister was still wanting foreign investment; British factories were operating successfully; we had done what we could to revive trade in Egyptian cotton by reopening the Alexandria-Liverpool market in cotton 'futures'; an agreement had been signed for the orderly liquidation of the Egyptian sterling balances; British exports to Egypt were again running at about £30 million a year, though Egyptian exports to Britain were only about £10 million; Shell were still refining and marketing Egyptian and imported, including Russian, oil, though their new drilling concession had arrived on Nasser's table for final signature on the day after a fierce campaign against him had started in the British Press and had consequently disappeared into thin air. There would be many difficulties; prospects for increasing trade were not great; but something could be done; there was something solid on which to build. For one month from 19 June to 19 July there was a lull. When Nehru arrived, I said to him: 'If you have any influence on Nasser, please tell him to keep quiet for a bit, to stop pushing and pressing.'

8

O N 26 July 1956, I visited the contractors at Tel el
Kebir. It was a difficult moment. The American and
British Governments had withdrawn their offers to
help finance the High Dam. Nasser had violently
attacked the Americans in a public speech. He was to
make an important speech that evening at Alexandria.
I was asked what I expected. I replied that we must
expect a violent attack on the West, in reply to the
withdrawal of the High Dam offer. I did not foresee that
Nasser would nationalise the Suez Canal Company at
this time. We had expected that the Western action
would be followed by Communist aid to build the dam.
Egyptian tactics had been to undermine the Company's
position, but not to make a frontal attack. We flashed
the news to London. I said to a member of my staff:
'Go round to the Company's office and see whether the
Police are in yet.' He found them just arriving on the
doorstep.

British politicians used at this time to say that Nasser
had seized the Canal at the point of the sword. This was
not correct. The Canal had always been under Egyptian jurisdiction and its security had throughout been
in Egyptian hands. France, supported by Russia, Germany and Austria Hungary, had tried to international-

ise the Canal in 1885, but had been prevented by the British in Egyptian interests. Nasser did not violate the 1888 Convention. He did not demand payment of dues in Egypt. Ships continued to pass freely through the Canal. He claimed that the Company was an Egyptian Company which he had the right to nationalise. International lawyers declared that the Company with its seat in Paris, its establishment under French law and its 'universal' character, was an international body with a special régime, subject to Egyptian law only in matters which did not conflict with its character, and not a Company which could be nationalised by the Egyptian Government under Egyptian 'municipal' law. But the matter was by no means clear. Some years before, in a case before the Mixed Courts, as Dr Fawzi pointed out to me, the lawyer for the British Government had claimed that it was an ordinary Egyptian national Company, without universal character, since this supported the British Government's case. Dr Fawzi omitted, however, to add that the Court, presided over by an Egyptian, found that the British Government's claim was invalid and that the Company's 'universal' title did comport a special legal character.

It soon appeared that the claim that nationalisation was a breach of an international agreement was not considered to rest solidly either solely on the Concession and the Company's international character or solely on the 1888 Convention. The argument was developed that it was a breach of the total régime established by the Concession read with the 1888 Convention, the preamble of which made it clear that the Convention was based on the Concession. This seemed to us in Cairo a better statement of the case, though weakened by the fact that the Convention was to continue in existence after the expiry of the Concession in 1968. The act of nationalisation was, in our opinion, a clear infringement of Egyptian 'municipal' law, which did not per-

mit the cancellation of concessions expiring on a fixed
date. But to raise this contention would be tantamount
to admitting that it was a question of Egyptian law,
which could be amended by the Egyptian Government.
Whatever the rights and wrongs of the legal position,
it was soon clear that neither side was going to base its
case on legal arguments nor seek a ruling from the
International Court. We had a good reason for not
going to the Court. Egypt had not signed the clause
binding it to accept the Court's jurisdiction in international disputes. It was not reasonable therefore to
let Egypt choose in which cases she would or would
not accept the Court's jurisdiction. The legal arguments were never important. It was a political issue.

Egyptian propagandists had labelled the Company as
a relic of the period of imperialist exploitation. They
had added for good measure that the Canal had been
built by the sacrifice of the lives of hundreds of thousands of Egyptian labourers, thus confusing De Lesseps
with the Pharaohs. They had accused the Company of
failing to employ enough Egyptians in responsible
positions. The Egyptian Government's aim had apparently been to ensure that well before the end of the
Concession, the Canal should be virtually run by
Egyptians. They pressed the Company to employ a
majority of Egyptian pilots. The Company resisted.
They wanted to keep the standards high and demanded
some years' experience as Master or Senior Officer of
a merchant ship at sea; but Egypt had no merchant
navy and Egyptian naval officers had little seamanship
and little sea experience. The Egyptian Government
also pressed for more positions in the management. The
Egyptian Directors were from the old régime. The
management body in Paris, which really ran the Company, was mainly French and the Company were determined to keep the Egyptians out of it. The Egyptian
Government also tried to extract as much foreign

exchange as possible from the Company. The main question had been whether the Company was subject to the Egyptian exchange control regulations. They kept the foreign exchange received from canal dues not only for their foreign exchange obligations but also for investment outside Egypt as a general reserve. The Egyptians demanded that the whole of the Company's foreign exchange should be invested in Egypt. The Company resisted and were determined to ensure that any settlement reached should not compromise their claim to special status carrying with it exemption from the automatic application of Egyptian legislation.

After long arguments an agreement was reached that the Company would continue to be exempt from exchange control until the end of the Concession in exchange for the investment of about £21 million in Egypt in the next few years. As soon as the agreement was signed, the Egyptians tried to get round it by proposing that the canal dues from British ships should be paid in Egyptian currency, the equivalent amount of sterling being reserved in a special account for the purchase of British goods. We refused. The Company agreed that some Egyptians without the required qualifications or experience would be employed as pilots. The Egyptian Commander in Chief demanded that the Company should develop a port at Ismailia, as provided in the Concession. This would give the Army new facilities for the transport of supplies over the Canal. No one took this seriously. The need for a harbour had been removed fifty years before by the development of Port Said. The demand for a share in the management in Paris remained unsettled.

From the beginning of 1956 the need to enlarge, perhaps to double the Canal, was under discussion. The Egyptian Government was approached by American oil companies and talked about it generally with the President of the International Bank when he was in

Cairo for the High Dam negotiations. Dr Fawzi told the American and French Ambassadors and me about these conversations. He said that this work would be an opportunity for co-operation between the Western Powers and the Egyptian Government. The Egyptian Government wanted the work to start as soon as possible and would not wish to encroach in any way on the Company's rights under the Concession. On the contrary, they wished to keep the closest and most friendly relations with the Company during the remaining period of the Concession. I did not forget this remark. The Company could finance its eighth works programme from its own funds. The ninth programme would require about £120 million, which would be financed partly from loans. We considered that the finance should be found from the International Bank which should be given a lien on future Canal revenues as security. Clearly, it would be impossible to negotiate a long-term loan without knowing something about the administration of the canal after the end of the Concession in 1968. This question would have to be considered in detail at latest by 1960. The Company commissioned an engineering and financial survey.

Nationalisation was described by the Western Press as the act of an irresponsible dictator in a tantrum, hitting out blindly against those whom he believed to have hurt him. Nasser clearly took this as an insult. His friend, Mohammed Hassanein Heikal, defended him on the lines that it was far from being a hasty decision but had been for a long time settled policy, and that Nasser had only waited for the right time. Nasser's long term policy was to nationalise all foreign and many indigenous enterprises. Nationalisation of the Canal Company had doubtless been under consideration since the early days of the Revolution. There were, however, good reasons against it. The Concession would come to an end in 1968. So long as Egypt had hopes of substantial aid from the West, it would not be worth their while to undertake all the risks of nationalisation with the certain loss of Western aid. In particular, while Western co-operation was to be given for the High Dam, the game was not worth the candle. It was better to pursue the alternative policy of trying to get into a position in which the Canal Company could not carry on without Egyptian co-operation, to infiltrate into the management and to squeeze out of the Company as much foreign exchange as possible. The requirement of the Company for finance from the International Bank for the enlargement of the Canal for a period extending beyond the period of the Concession, coupled with the interest of the oil and shipping companies and the Governments of the Maritime Powers in the administration of the Canal after the end of the Concession, might make it possible to obtain an agreement for the early termination of the Concession in return for the establishment of a permanent Canal administration which would meet Egyptian requirements and satisfy the needs of the Canal users.

Up till the spring of 1956 the arguments against nationalisation were surely the stronger. But the atmosphere was then changing. We know that Nasser noted the views of a Conservative back-bencher, expressed in a debate on the adjournment in March, that Nasser was not fit to have control of the Canal after 1968. We know that by June Nasser was expecting the withdrawal of the High Dam offer, as we were, and that he was already contemplating nationalisation of the Company in retaliation. We know that Colonel Zachariya Mohieddin was carrying out staff studies on it some weeks before the announcement. If Nasser was not going to get Western aid for the High Dam, the Canal revenues would help towards it. In 1957 Nasser in one of his anniversary speeches, linked the act of nationalisation with the financing of the Dam. By July 1956, the Western Powers were showing extreme hostility. Nasser was probably assured of Soviet political support and Soviet aid for the dam, if the West gave up. So it must have appeared by that time that the balance of advantage had tipped the other way. Nasser was always a gambler. He was now ready to gamble for the highest stakes.

9

I KNEW Nasser in a transitional period, when it was already apparent that his aims would clash with British interests, when the British occupation was at its end and the new Egypt, confident and ambitious, was seeking to play a greater part in the world. Nasser regarded himself as the destined champion of Arab nationalism. His basic ideas were set out in his pamphlet 'The Philosophy of the Revolution'. There were to be two revolutions, the political, to get rid of the King and the occupation, and the social, starting with land reform. Every country must look beyond its boundaries to find its rôle in the world. Egypt had to take account of three circles, Arab, which was the most important, African and Islamic. In the region in which the Egyptians lived, there was a rôle seeking an actor to play it. The source of Arab power was Arab unity, Egypt's strategic position and oil. Imperialism supporting Israel was the foremost force opposing the Arabs. Egypt could not stand aside from the struggle between the Africans and Whites in Africa. Egypt had a responsibility to diffuse civilisation in the African jungle and the Nile was the artery of Egyptian life. The leaders of the Moslem States, meeting in regular political congress, should draw up the main lines of Islamic policy and co-operation.

At this time, Nasser was at heart still a revolutionary conspirator. Having been successful in Egypt, he stirred

things up all over the Middle East in furtherance of the
revolutionary aims which he regarded as justifying his
action. I am inclined to believe the story that, when
reproached in 1957 with the inept conspiracies conducted by his military attachés, he replied with charac-
teristic humour that the poor boys were so impulsive;
it was difficult to restrain them. He told me that he had
been a conspirator for so long that he thought like one
and was suspicious of everyone. I tried to persuade him
that he would achieve more by showing a little more
confidence in others. He replied that he might perhaps
be able to do so in a few years' time, but not yet. He
did not trust most of his officials. He told me that
foreign agents could find out nothing from his immediate circle, since he and his friends never wrote
anything down. The one man from outside his immediate circle whom he appeared to trust completely was
Dr Fawzi.

He showed self-confidence, courage and nervous
control. He was willing to take great risks. In May 1956
he said to me: 'You cannot carry out a gunboat policy
against me as you could against Farouk. I have no
throne, no hereditary position, no fortune.' In October
1956 he told a British correspondent that if he were
attacked, he would pull down the pillars of the house
like Samson and that in preparation for an attack he
had set up a guerrilla organisation, the members of
which would be required to kill within twenty-four
hours any President or Prime Minister appointed by a
British military Commander. Neguib, in his apologia,
wrote that Nasser believed in taking more risks than
he thought wise. In the early days before and after the
revolution, Nasser was in his element. He loved to
dwell on those times, when everything was simple for
him, subordinated to one purpose. He talked for hours
on the preparations for the plot, originally timed for
1955, the planting of his agents among the enemy, the

swift execution of the plot, the complicated manoeuvres designed to make Neguib overplay his hand. He painted vivid pictures; how the Salem brothers had flown from Alexandria to urge him to try the King and execute him and how he had refused, saying that a revolution which begins in blood ends in blood; how he had proposed that Neguib should not be allowed to resign, but that the whole revolutionary council should resign and show him that he could not get on without them, and had been overruled; how, while the crowd were hailing Neguib at the Abdin Palace, he withdrew the police and then telephoned to Neguib that he was not in control and risked Cairo being burnt again. One day, at the end of an hour's story of the negotiations with Neguib, I said: 'We must get on with some work; but I hope to hear the end of the story another time.' He replied: 'It has not ended yet and I wonder how it will end.'

Nasser showed great tactical skill and thought out his tactics carefully. In his speech announcing the nationalisation of the Suez Canal Company, he said: 'We used different methods to secure the evacuation of the British Occupation Forces. We combined violence with leniency and negotiation.' The pattern of action during the Suez affair was the same. But he did not always see where his tactics were leading him. Nor did he see that he would fail in his external aims since it was beyond the power of his country to support them.

Nasser was admittedly an opportunist. 'Really, I have no plan,' was one of his favourite remarks. He had, at that time, little experience of the outside world or of international affairs. His reading was almost exclusively the Press, principally the foreign Press, which he read every night from midnight until he went to bed, remembering, as he once told me, only the bad bits, from over-suspiciousness deriving ideas about the policies of other Governments which were sometimes way off the mark. He seemed unwilling to distinguish between the relative value as an indication of the British Government's policy, of a statement by a Minister in the House of Commons, the casual interjections of a back bencher in revolt against Ministers and snippets in the gossip columns of the popular Press, though this may have sometimes been a conscious misrepresentation.

He was an adept in the technique used by other politicians in answering awkward questions. He would take great care not to say anything which could be proved to be literally untrue. He would answer the question which had not been put. He would use for his own purposes material of doubtful accuracy, such as the French list of British arms supplied to Israel, after I had told him that it bore no relation to the facts. His explanations of his actions were ingenious, but not always convincing. He used to say that he was not attacking the British in the Middle East. Propaganda attacks were either not in accordance with his instructions or were justifiable as a counter-attack against propaganda attacks on him. His argument implied that if British interests suffered from the pursuit of his aims which were impeccable – liberty and independence for the Arab States, the increase of Egyptian power and influence as a foundation for Arab unity – it was for the British to understand, not condemn. But, though he concealed much, he could be remarkably frank. He liked to represent himself as a misunderstood man. He was fond of saying that he was in the position of a man unjustly sentenced for a murder which he had not committed, to a prison sentence of fifteen years, who, coming out of prison, sees walking along the street the man whom he was supposed to have murdered and promptly shoots him. Why, he would say, was he accused of so much for which he was not responsible? He only wished he had the organisation to do half of what he was accused.

Nasser was one of the large family of a minor Post Office official in an Egypt of glaring social and economic inequality and felt bitterly towards members of the old régime. He told me that he knew none of the Pasha class and that, during his first visit to the Gezira Club, he had felt so uncomfortable that he had never gone there again. His belief in the need for social and economic reform was, I feel sure, quite genuine. I have no reason to doubt that he was a sincere Moslem. He seemed to believe in the possibility of direct divine intervention. He related to me the story which he had told in his pamphlet. He had tried to commit a political murder. Horrified by the screams of the victim's wife, he had prayed all night that the man would survive. His prayers had been answered. He had a happy family life. His wife, the modest daughter of an Iranian carpet dealer, devoted herself to her husband and her four children. Nasser told me once that his wife had been worried during the period of his conspiracy by his frequent absences at night, but did not worry any more, once she knew that he was out on secret business and not after women. My wife, whom Madame Nasser said was the first Englishwoman whom she had met, found her a genuine, kindly and friendly person, unconcerned with politics. They lived modestly in a house in Abbasia, which had formerly been a British Major's house, though enlarged for them. Nasser played tennis, but gave it up for a time during the mounting stress of 1956. He relaxed by retreating to the Nile barrage, seven miles from Cairo, or by frequent summer visits to Bourg el Arab, near the sea, thirty miles from Alexandria on the road to Alamein.

Nasser had considerable personal charm and was always apparently relaxed. He never lost his temper or raised his voice in conversation. He had no difficulty in making people feel at their ease. If he showed fanaticism in his speeches, it was a studied and controlled effect, however strong the emotion behind it. If he had been a lesser man, interested only in his own power or the material advantages which power brings, he would have been easier to deal with; but he was a visionary, whose visions could not be reconciled with British interests in the Arab world and who was apt to identify his own ambitions with the will of Providence. His restless activity outside Egypt, excused by the bland assertion that Egypt could not be indifferent to the area surrounding it, his tendency to overplay his hand, to push too hard, his love of conspiracy, coupled with our failure to realise the changes in the Arab world and the effect of our relative loss of power, landed both countries in trouble.

Nasser made the revolution with his small circle of fellow conspirators, all Army or Air Officers. His closest and most loyal friend seemed to be General Hakim Amer, Commander of the Armed Forces, agreeable, not quick-witted, a devotee of Agatha Christie's novels, whose sudden death in 1967 is outside the scope of this narrative. The most intelligent was Colonel Zachariya Mohieddin, Minister of the Interior, who appeared to us to be the only member of the circle with the capacity to succeed Nasser and who, we felt, though without any firm evidence, was a little too clever to have Nasser's unreserved confidence. The two Salem brothers were too excitable and unpredictable to last for long. Gamal, the elder, a sick man, faded out after his marriage. Salah, the 'dancing major', as the British Press nicknamed him, had a chequered career, dismissed from his post as Minister, appointed editor of a newspaper created for him, under house arrest after Suez, and died young. The rest were of less account. It seems that only one or two are still in the picture.

Of the civilian Ministers, Dr Fawzi, the Foreign Minister, was a good professional, very intelligent, with an attractive personality, a strong but moderate nationalist whom I personally liked very much, and who, I still think, tried to stop the slide downhill. He was subtle and indirect in his approach and was on especially good terms with Dag Hammarskjöld, whose methods were somewhat similar and who probably overestimated Fawzi's influence with Nasser at that time. In the domain of foreign affairs, he has remained in position, but not always in power. I used to visit him often in riding clothes in his country house on the Sakkara road and we used to go over our problems, though in the end we failed to find the way through all the tangles of those times. The other civilian Ministers were men of technical ability, but without influence on policy.

Egyptians are not noticeably partial to their leaders and Nasser cannot be said to have been popular inside his own country. But there was no serious challenge to his authority. The minorities and the traders grumbled, but in those days were still able to make and enjoy substantial fortunes. Their troubles were still to come. The old landowners bitterly resented the expropriation of most of their land, but could still make about £80 an acre out of the two hundred acres which they were then allowed to keep, and continued to live in great comfort in Cairo or Alexandria in the winter and in Europe in the summer, until the Government began to restrict their movement out of Egypt in the summer of 1956. They had no political support. If there had been free elections, the Wafd would have swept the board, but they could not raise their heads.

The Armed Forces were the principal support of the régime. The officers were treated as a favoured class and given houses, cars and refrigerators on easy terms. The older officers were probably not fully trusted. In the summer of 1956 a large number of them were retired and replaced by younger men. The Police, traditionally opposed to the army, seemed to be loyal and well-disciplined. In 1956 Nasser began to replace the older type of civil official, who mostly came from the class which had little sympathy for the revolution, with Army Officers, who were inserted into key positions in the Ministries. The industrial workers supported the Government. The fellahin were only interested in the few requirements of their hard lives, good cotton prices and cheap consumer goods. They had been benefited by land reform.

Security was good. There were no student demonstrations and the local Communists and Muslim Brotherhood were effectively suppressed. There were detention camps and the Police were probably not gentle; but we had no evidence that the revolutionary Government were any tougher in dealing with their opponents than the old régime had been. Corruption was checked but still reached near, though not to the top. Nasser used the Press as a political weapon. In the summer of 1956 censorship was formally lifted; but this made no practical difference. Each newspaper had a Government representative on its staff and was compelled to follow the Government line and to print articles inspired by the Government. One of the most serious losses suffered by Egypt as a result of the revolution, was the transformation of its independent newspapers into organs of the Government propaganda machine.

Nasser used to talk to me about the gradual development of the constitution. For perhaps five years, there would be one party, then two for another five years; then perhaps any number could be allowed. Complete freedom would lead to a Communist victory. He made it clear that he intended to exclude his political opponents from Parliament. He said he had thought for a long time how to manage the elections. He could allow complete freedom of nomination and then ensure the election of the Government candidate, or he could exclude undesirable candidates and then allow free elections between the pre-selected candidates. He had

chosen the second method. It was the basic problem
of the dictator trying to give the appearance of a par-
liamentary system, but at the same time keeping the
power firmly in his own hands. In the event, Egyptian
politics went in the expected way, a plebiscite, in which
a few actually voted against or abstained, a single party
composed of pre-selected candidates and controlled
elections, opposition to the Government making itself
felt by intrigues within the Government, students' riots
and plots by the Communists or Muslim Brotherhood.

Nasser presumably took it for granted that I should
be intriguing against him and had me elaborately
watched, though my guards were also there to protect
me from assassination which might be contrived by
his opponents to get him into trouble. Sir Lee Stack and
Lord Moyne were not forgotten. When I went outside
my gate on foot, I was accompanied by four policemen,
dispersed round me like fielders at cricket. I had a car
in front of and one behind my car, though I soon
managed to get rid of the car in front and, until the
tensions of the autumn of 1956, was able to dispense
also with the other car when going to ride or play tennis
in the afternoons, though I knew that there was a plain-
clothes policeman at the Ghiza stables. Towards the end,
a mounted policeman came with me on rides, when
Nasser seemed to think that even the British Government might stage an incident against me to create
provocation justifying British action.

Suspicion of my doings was shown particularly when
I used occasionally to go to the Ekkiad shoot over the
desert in General Hull's jeep, where the Police car
could not go. Then Colonel Zachariya had me well
clocked out and clocked in at the other end, in order to
check that I was not dallying in the intervening desert
for a political meeting, as I told him. The 'anges guar-
diens', as my Police were nicknamed by the diplomatic
colleagues, were most friendly, though rather embar-

rassing if one wanted to be sick on the desert, and liable to collide with the back of the Embassy car, since the authorities provided them with sten guns but no brakes. Visitors to the house were reported, but that did not seem to prevent plenty of Egyptians from coming in.

10

VIOLENT reactions in London and New York, speeches by the Prime Minister and the Foreign Secretary declaring Nasser the enemy, the London Conference, blocking of Egyptian balances in London, Paris and New York, calling-up of the British and French Reserves; Nasser's act of nationalisation had transformed the situation. H.M.S. *Jamaica*, on a good-will visit to Egypt, sailed away. There was no good will left. I could do no business with Egyptian Ministers. I could not discuss the nationalisation of the Company, since it was being handled by Governments which showed no disposition to negotiate with the Egyptians. A request to see Nasser would be taken as a sign of weakness, and I had no instructions.

Throughout this period I saw only two Ministers. Some minor electrical work was being carried out at the contractors' ammunition depot. The Police suspected preparations for sabotage. They picked on an old wartime saboteur employed in the Shell Refinery. He was playing billiards with a friend. They arrested the wrong man. He telephoned to enquire. They arrested him too and deported both. I protested to the Minister of the Interior. The Minister took it calmly. They had been arrested for security reasons. It was the leave season. They could return when it became cooler. Then he started on politics, which gave me my opportunity. I said that the revolutionary Government had made the biggest mistake of their career. They needed friends, but had lost them by their own actions. They should not think that this was a little trouble which would blow over. The British regarded it as a matter which affected their vital interests. The Egyptian Government had destroyed foreign confidence in the régime. Who would now want to invest in Egypt? They were clinging to an old-fashioned concept of sovereignty which had no meaning in the conditions of the modern world. The only people who now claimed to be their friends were the Communists, and they would find that the Communists were not their real friends, but were only using them for their own purposes. The Menzies Mission were about to come to Cairo to communicate to Nasser the proposals of the eighteen countries at the London Conference. They should accept these proposals and make an effort to repair this serious breach in their relations with the Western world. The Minister said little but that history would judge whether they were right or wrong.

The Foreign Office suggested that I repeat this elsewhere. I would not ask for an interview with Nasser. So I went to see Dr Fawzi in his house outside Cairo. I spoke on the same lines. I reminded him of his statement about the Egyptian Government's desire for co-operation with the Canal Company and respect for its rights under the Concession. I had started by asking him to listen to my personal views. With some he would disagree. With others he might agree, but would not be able to say so. When he had heard me, I should not expect him to comment. We could talk about the garden. He heard me in silence. When I had finished, he pointed to a flower-bed and said: 'Over there, you will see a most curious flower. . . .' I did not see him again until the third week of October.

Nasser could have done it in a very different way. He could have summoned the Company's representative, told him of the decision, arranged for the Company's property to be handed over and proposed an international tribunal to discuss compensation. He chose the violent way, a gesture of defiance, attacking the British, the French and the Company, announcing as a final decision the basis of the compensation which he was prepared to offer if the Company would hand over to him all their foreign assets and seizing the Company's property by force. He followed his act of violence by careful moderation. He hardly made a public speech throughout the crisis. Retaliatory measures against British interests were hastily rescinded. The Western Powers made no attempt to negotiate with him and he was therefore relieved from having to agree to a compromise. The invitation to him to attend the London Conference was explicitly stated to be on the basis that the act of nationalisation was illegal. As we expected, he refused it. He said afterwards that he would have accepted the invitation without commitment if it had not been for the Prime Minister's personal attack on him at that moment. I doubted this, though, if he had had a mind to go, the speech would certainly have stopped him.

He received the Menzies Mission and talked to them; but they had no mandate to negotiate and he could not have accepted their proposals without appearing to give in completely and so destroying his position in Egypt and the rest of the Arab world. He demanded that the Canal should be under Egyptian management. The Western Powers demanded that it should be under international management. At this stage, neither were prepared to compromise. The Menzies Mission was not helped by a statement made by President Eisenhower while they were in Cairo, that whatever happened, force must not be used. This greatly upset Mr Menzies. Mr Loy Henderson, the American representative, felt that it was ill-timed and strengthened Nasser's hand. But it was not crucial at this point. Nasser would not have given way in any case to the Western demand that he reverse his position.

The Canal Company believed that they could dislocate Canal traffic by withdrawing their pilots. Nasser had taken power to prosecute pilots who refused to work and let it be known that he would do so if there were a mass walk-out. It was important not to give him the chance of accusing the British and French Governments of conniving with the Company to break the 1888 Convention. The Company's agents were putting it out in the Canal area that the two Governments were planning to withdraw the pilots and stop navigation in the Canal. The Governments decided that if they withdrew the pilots before the Menzies Mission arrived in Cairo, they could not claim that they were making a reasonable proposal which Nasser should accept. They therefore decided to postpone the date for the withdrawal of the pilots until the middle of September. In the meanwhile, the pilots were asked to register their loyalty to the Company in a document to be signed before the British and French Consuls. The Company's advice to them was limited to telling them that the two Governments no longer found it necessary to ask them to stay at their posts after the date fixed. They could then decide for themselves what to do. This safeguarded the position of the Governments under the 1888 Convention.

It was now fairly certain that most of the pilots would leave when told to by the Company. They knew that the advice had the backing of Governments. The Company had made generous offers of compensation to those who registered. They were increasingly doubtful about their prospects under an Egyptian Canal Authority.

But we reported our opinion that although the withdrawal of the pilots would cause difficulties to the new Authority and perhaps delays, it would not stop the passage of ships through the Canal. New Egyptian and foreign pilots were being recruited. Their training would be brief and their standard would not be high; but they could probably do the job in most conditions. The Western shipping companies were already routeing their biggest ships round the Cape. The average tanker or freighter Captain knew the Canal so well that he could take his ship through without a pilot. It was the easy season. The Company's pilots were no exception to the general rule that experts overvalue their importance. And so it fell out. The pilots left. Nasser prudently let them go without taking punitive action against them which might have formed a pretext for Western retaliation by force. The Canal administration went on, not very well at first, but without any obvious deterioration of service. We then thought that in course of time there would be a gradual lowering of efficiency as a result of which many ships would avoid the Canal. This did not happen. The Egyptian administration proved very efficient.

Ministers and diplomats continued to fly round the world, conferring, arguing and making statements, but it all seemed to have little to do with anything that happened in Cairo. The Menzies Mission, which had impinged on us, was followed by the second conference of the 'users', the formation of the 'users'' association and the realisation that the S.C.U.A., the skewer as we called it, had a blunt point. The Egyptians recalled to me later that when asked what would happen if the Egyptians denied the 'users' passage through the Canal, Sir Anthony Eden replied that they would force their way through. When Mr Dulles was asked the same question, he replied that they would go round the Cape. We had been asked, in common with other Middle East posts, whether time was or was not on our side. We replied that it was not. Nasser had, it appeared, won a diplomatic victory by sitting tight and demonstrating that his opponents could do nothing by their conferences and journeys round the world. He had shown that he could keep the Canal open without the pilots. No Egyptian liked the Suez Canal Company, and if Nasser could pull off his coup, almost everyone in Egypt would applaud him. The initial doubters were coming round to his side, since he was doing well. Inside Egypt genuine patriotism had been stimulated by the presence of British and French troops near at hand and by the formation of a 'Home Guard' to 'defend the fatherland'. One of the less bright ideas which was canvassed at this time in the British Press was that we should cut off the Nile water at the Owen Falls dam. There were plenty of reasons why we should not do this. It would rouse the fellahin against us and behind Nasser. It would hurt the Sudanese peasants too. It would only affect a small proportion of the water which the Nile brought down to Egypt. We poured cold water on it.

Later, the situation began to turn against Nasser. About the end of September there were signs that Jordan and Saudi Arabia were beginning to move away from him towards Iraq. Even Syria did not seem so secure an ally as hitherto. The restrictions on Egyptian sterling began to have some effect. The outcome of the struggle looked more obscure. It seemed that the threat to Egypt might be prolonged. The Egyptians began to show signs of nervousness. Arms were widely distributed and preparations were made for guerrilla warfare. Egyptians could read in the British Press of the movement of Egyptian block-ships towards the Canal. Tension was rising. The Indians were pressing Nasser to settle. The British and French clearly had no intention of giving way. They were putting the matter to the

Security Council. At the beginning of October I reported that, as it appeared in Cairo, the situation had moved in our favour, and if the matter were to be settled by negotiation, the near future would be a favourable moment. The threat from the British and French Forces was now having its effect. An Arab colleague took the view that if the British and French let Nasser have his way, all non-Communists would suffer. If they used force, the consequences would be disastrous. In either case, only the Communists would benefit. But on no account should the British and the French take their Forces away until the affair was settled.

The debates in the Security Council in the first half of October and the concurrent private meetings between Mr Selwyn Lloyd, Monsieur Pineau and Dr Fawzi, made it appear to us in Cairo that both sides were at last preparing to negotiate. I felt that there was now little chance that force would be used against Egypt. The early opportunity had been missed. Nasser was giving no provocation and there was a clear division of opinion on the use of force in Britain. I judged, wrongly, that force would not be used without overwhelming political support at home. By the middle of October the Security Council had approved the six principles which were to govern the detailed arrangements for management of the Canal. I called on Dr Fawzi on his return from New York. He was cautious, but relatively hopeful. Mr Hammarskjöld had proposed a meeting of the three Foreign Ministers at Geneva on 29 October, to negotiate within the framework of the six principles. Dr Fawzi told me that he was convinced that Mr Selwyn Lloyd had sincerely tried for an agreement in New York, though Monsieur Pineau had not. He said that the Egyptians were ready to go to Geneva on the 29th and would be glad to know whether the two Governments also were ready to go. Mr Selwyn Lloyd had made a public statement that the British Government could not negotiate unless the Egyptian Government first made detailed proposals as a basis for negotiation. This, said Dr Fawzi, was unreasonable. Egypt could not be asked to write the Treaty before the negotiation began.

In October I wrote to Sir Ivone Kirkpatrick, the Permanent Under Secretary at the Foreign Office, that it seemed that we were now approaching the stage of negotiations over the Canal. I thought that there was much to be said for preliminary negotiations being conducted through normal diplomatic channels. If negotiations were seriously contemplated, should I not return home for consultations? I had not been out of Egypt since January. He replied that he had been thinking for some time of asking the Secretary of State to call me to London for consultations, but that the situation was still fluid and it would be better to wait and see how it developed.

On 30 October I was asked to see Dr Fawzi to receive a protest that R.A.F. Canberras had invaded Egyptian air space. After getting this complaint off his chest, Dr Fawzi turned to the Canal question. He said that the date of 29 October had now passed. The British Government's attitude in demanding a draft Treaty in advance of negotiations was, he feared, only an excuse to avoid negotiation altogether. He had now received a letter from the Secretary General giving his understanding of the negotiations in New York and filling out the points discussed there. He was not yet sure how he would answer this letter. He could not accept it, since he had certain reservations on parts of it. But it could be placed on the table as a basis for negotiation by the three Governments in the presence of the Secretary General, without commitment on either side. He considered that we had reached a crucial stage in the matter and that he and I should keep in close touch over the next few weeks. He even revived his familiar theme that the Canal would form a solid basis for future co-operation between Egypt and the West; but that I rejected as totally ignoring all that had happened since 26 July. A few hours later the ultimatum was delivered.

would find it difficult to withdraw their troops from the Canal and leave a foreign Company, imposed by force, without their protection. The lot of the employees left behind would not be enviable.

Whatever was done, we should not endanger the lives of the large non-Egyptian population in Cairo, in Alexandria and on the Canal. A breakdown of internal security in the cities might have most serious consequences for Egyptians and others, for which we should bear a heavy responsibility. There was the political aspect. The British and French could not continue their occupation indefinitely. They would have to leave again. If so, the Egyptians would create the myth that they had expelled the foreign Forces and liberated themselves. The British would again figure in the Egyptian school-books, this time not only as the aggressors, but as the aggressors defeated by the Egyptian heroes. When we looked back after the event, we could not think of anything more we could usefully have said. Nor am I now inclined to think that this assessment was wrong. Nasser said to me much later that the Egyptians spend their time blaming the Government and making up funny stories about it, but when their country is threatened, they unite to defend it.

Our main direct preoccupation was the British Community, their safety and their evacuation in advance of hostilities, if they were seriously planned. At the beginning of August, on instructions from London, we issued to the Community a warning that those whose presence in Egypt was not essential, should consider whether it was not in their best interests to leave, and that those on holiday at home should consider postponing their return. Some of the British Community did not take kindly to this warning. They remembered the similar warning issued in 1953, which in the light of what happened, they considered to have been unnecessary and to have been only a manoeuvre in political warfare.

They asked whether the British Embassy were sending away the dependents and less essential staff, and were told that we were not doing so, since Embassy Staffs were entitled by diplomatic practice to protection which other British subjects would not have. In fact, if security had broken down, this would not have meant much.

In talking to the British Community, we were in a difficulty. Local security was excellent. Nasser was being very careful to see that there was no local incident which would support the belief that British lives were in danger, in view of the British Government's statement that they were calling up the Reserves in order to protect British lives. The British Community knew well enough that the only threat to their lives and property would come from British action, which would result in the breakdown of the Egyptian Security Services. With some grumbling, the Community accepted the advice in fairly large numbers. It was repeated in the same terms at the end of August and again in the middle of September, when there were signs that some of the families thought that they had been away long enough and wanted to come back.

We expected to be left with about two thousand English, the community being already depleted by the warnings and the summer holiday season, about seven thousand Maltese and rather fewer Cypriots. We made contingency plans for the evacuation of the remaining community in two stages, in the event of real trouble looming ahead. We hoped to reduce it to the hard core in the first stage by issuing a serious warning and providing ships and aircraft to evacuate all who agreed to leave. In the second stage, if it should appear that hostilities could not be avoided, we should try and get the hard core out in time, though we realised that they might be left behind. We did not want to make any distinctions of race; but the different sections of the

British community would not suffer the same degree
of difficulties in an emergency. The Government of
Cyprus did not want an influx of Cypriots, many of
whom had been actively working against the British
Government in favour of Enosis. The majority of the
Maltese were born in Egypt and under the Maltese
regulations could not go to Malta. But they might be
in some danger in an emergency and want to leave.
The Home Office did not want a displaced persons'
problem in Britain. We got ready a warning to give
to individual English and to the leading Cypriots and
Maltese. We were authorised to help Maltese to leave,
but were asked to discourage them from doing so, except for those who might for special reason be in personal danger. This, in the circumstances, was fair
enough.

It was decided in London to send the teachers back
without their families for the new term in October.
The contractors' employees in the Canal zone were in
an exposed position. The London Board therefore with
the co-operation of the Egyptians, repatriated the
women employees, some of the men and all the families.
About four hundred and fifty men remained. All
through these months we reviewed the evacuation
problem continually with the Foreign Office, the British
community leaders and the B.O.A.C. All who wanted
to go, went by normal transport; but it eventually became clear that there could be no evacuation by official
means, since there would be no spare transport, and that
all who did not leave by normal means before an emergency arose, were liable to be left without means of
escape. We told this to the leaders of the British community.

My children had arrived for the summer holidays two
days after Nasser had nationalised the Company. They
stayed for three weeks in Alexandria. Life was normal
there, except for restrictions of access to some beaches,

the erection of defences of a sort and the appearance of
young peasants in Home Guard uniform. My wife and
a party of ladies of various nationalities were anchored
off shore near Aboukir, while the children swam to
shore and raced up and down the sand dunes. Suddenly
two young Home Guarders appeared, loaded their
rifles and lined the children up on the beach, pointing
a rifle at each child who moved. One boy was rowing
the dinghy. There was a moment of verbal contest between the Home Guarder urging him to the shore and
mother urging him to the yacht. He obeyed his mother
and the ladies were able to get to shore and parley, while
the nine children, ranging in age from seventeen to
seven, Egyptian, Greek, Lebanese and English, sat in
a row at the water's edge under guard. The affair ended
with the appearance of an officer who sent his young
enthusiasts packing. It was clearly wise to keep clear of
the Home Guard.

In Cairo life went on peacefully on the surface, but
under a cloud of apprehension. The British and French
families thinned out; rumours proliferated; social contacts with Egyptians practically ceased. The bazaar was
in a state of nerves; the Home Guard drilled every
evening on vacant lots; the Press tried every form of
abuse. Camps sprang up round the Pyramids. My military attaché, riding near one, was pulled off his horse
and the horse pulled down onto the ground. The horse
kicked, the soldiers backed hastily and he was able to
ride off without saying who he was. After that, we gave
the area a wide berth. We continued our afternoon
rides and our rides across the desert by moonlight to
Sakkara. For weeks Mars presented a warlike face,
blood red and looming large in the Eastern sky. Surely,
we thought, this must be a good omen; for the Heavens
would not foretell war in such an obvious way.

The Embassy families thinned out until the feminine
element in the Embassy was reduced to two wives, one

my own, and the secretaries. We decided that my wife should not leave before the secretaries. Some less essential male staff were posted elsewhere; two were expelled and two Egyptians were expelled from the Egyptian Embassy in London. Four British were arrested for spying. We made their life in prison as easy as possible and arranged for their defence. In the political atmosphere of the moment it was not in their interests to press for an early trial. A horde of British and American Press correspondents stayed in Cairo throughout the summer without much to do. The excitement took place outside; Cairo remained quite calm. One correspondent described it neatly as the still epicentre of a cyclone. One decided that three days in Cairo would be enough; so he wrote two articles so abusive of Nasser that he got himself expelled on the third day, which made a good story for his final article. Four bored correspondents tried to penetrate the house where General Neguib was under arrest and were expelled. General Neguib was removed out of harm's way, probably to Upper Egypt. We gave the correspondents such daily guidance as we could, though we had little enough to feed them on.

At the beginning of October the atmosphere seemed to lighten. Military intervention now seemed unlikely; the weather was cooler. We were getting used to the situation and started entertaining again, including some Egyptian friends. By the end of the month we began to look forward to some easing of the situation during the winter, though we expected that it would be a long haul before a settlement was found. We provisionally arranged a party to travel up the Nile to Luxor and beyond, and we fixed the weekend of 27 October to repay Alexandrian hospitality with a party at our house, which would show that if we stood on the edge of a precipice, we had not lost our balance.

When we returned from dining with friends on that Monday evening, I was given the news that the Israelis had attacked. A telegram arrived from Tel Aviv reporting that the Israeli Ministry of Defence had called in the British and French military attachés and told them that the Israeli Forces had attacked in Southern Sinai, while parachute Forces had been dropped a short distance East of Suez, their objective being Suez. On checking with my American colleague, now Mr Ray Hare, I heard to my surprise that he had not heard that the American military attaché in Tel Aviv had been given the same information by the Israelis. We thought: 'Thank God, that lets us out,' and 'Now we do have to get the British community out.' As soon as we had the telegram from Tel Aviv, I telegraphed to London asking whether I should now reduce the Embassy to the 'hard core', sending away my wife, the remaining two wives (one who had remained for special personal reasons and one who had returned on her own initiative without telling her husband), the secretaries and the men who could be spared without our shutting up shop.

At 1.30 a.m., I went to bed. I was woken at 2.30 a.m. by a telephone call from the B.O.A.C. representative who told me that the International Airport had been closed, that there were two British aircraft on the airport and that he hoped to get them away at dawn. At 4.30 a.m. I woke up my wife and told her that if she wanted to leave, this was probably the last opportunity until the fighting stopped. She replied: 'Don't be silly. I have a hair appointment in the morning and I am very sleepy.' I returned to bed. At 6.30 a.m. I received a telegram that I should send away everyone except the male 'hard core'. I told my wife that she must go, had the others informed and, with great difficulty, managed to reach the Egyptian Commander-in-Chief by telephone, since his orders were necessary for the aircraft to leave. He agreed that the aircraft could leave at

midday with the Embassy staff and any other British
who could get on them.

At 6.30 a.m. I had also received instructions to warn
all members of the British Community who might be in
danger, to leave. I delivered the message personally to
the leading members of the British Community at 9
a.m., the earliest time by which they could be assembled.
I had also immediately instructed the Consuls outside
Cairo to deliver similar warnings to the British Community in their districts. A small committee was
immediately set up to co-ordinate action between the
Embassy and the Community, to assist evacuation. They
were well aware that I had no instructions and no means
to organise their evacuation and that I could do no
more than try, with them, to ensure that the means of
transport which existed, would be used to the best
possible advantage.

At 10.30 a.m. the Americans told me that Nasser's
friend had been with them and had protested vigorously
against the intrusion of R.A.F. Canberras over Egyptian
air-space and soon afterwards I received a request from
Dr Fawzi to see him at 12.30 p.m. It took a long time
to round up the girls with their luggage. Four girls had
to be left behind. We reserved passages for a hundred
and five of the Staff on the next two ships leaving
Alexandria.

At 12.30 p.m. I saw Dr Fawzi who made his protest
about the Canberras. I took the opportunity to deliver
a Note which I had been instructed on the previous day
to give him, informing the Egyptian Government of the
intention of Her Majesty's Government to withdraw
the contractors from the Suez Canal Base without
prejudice to the rights of Her Majesty's Government
under the Base Agreement and the eventual resumption of the exercise of those rights. Dr Fawzi accepted
the position stated in the Note and we arranged that
the details should be discussed by members of our

Staffs. The same afternoon an agreed Minute was drawn up ad referendum to the two Governments, making arrangements for the temporary hand-over of the Base installations to the Egyptian Government. At 6 p.m. I was working in my office when a member of my Staff came in and said: 'I think you had better come down the corridor and see what is coming in over the ticker.' It was the British Government's ultimatum, which had presumably been delivered to the Egyptian Ambassador in London, since it had not been delivered through me.

I was asked to see Nasser at 9 p.m. Dr Fawzi was with him. I was determined not to be less self-possessed than he was. I opened by saying that I was grateful to General Hakim Amer for having agreed to the British aircraft leaving. Nasser said: 'I have not seen you for a long time.' I replied: 'No. It is your fault. You did not ask me to come. The last time we met was, I think, on 18 June, with General Robertson.' 'No,' he replied, priding himself, as usual, on his memory for detail; 'It was 19 June and I saw you again on 19 July.' I replied: 'Yes, you are right. I was not counting the time on the airport, when Nehru was leaving.' He said: 'Now I have your ultimatum.' I replied: 'I have the text which I have just received. Dr Fawzi will realise that I knew nothing of it this afternoon when we had our discussion.' This I felt bound to say, since, if I had known at that time that an ultimatum was just about to be given, I should have spoken very differently. I went on: 'But it does not say it is an ultimatum. It says, "Communication".' Nasser replied: 'We take it as an ultimatum.' He then gave the Egyptian Government's reply. He said that it was a threat of unprovoked aggression, without any justification. Here I interposed: 'According to my text, the purpose of the intervention is to stop the fighting and protect the Canal.' Nasser replied: 'We can defend the Canal and tomorrow we shall be defending it from more than the Israelis.' I told him that I should communicate his reply to Her Majesty's Government. I relied on him to protect the Embassy and British lives and property. Nasser gave his assurance that he would do so.

As usual at the end of an interview, Nasser pressed the bell. Five photographers came in. The photograph published in the Egyptian Press was of my turning on my heel while Nasser and Dr Fawzi grinned at each other like schoolboys who have just put a tintack on the master's chair. Nasser was completely at ease throughout. There is a photograph of my leaving the Presidency. I am passing in front of the Embassy Rolls with the Union Jack visible. Leaning over the balcony above, one of Nasser's A.D.C.s looks down at me, half grinning, half frightened, like a gargoyle on the keystone of a medieval arch.

The British Government's time limit for the withdrawal of the Egyptian Forces from the Canal was due to expire at 4 a.m. on 31 October. I expected to wake up and find the Embassy surrounded, but everything was normal. Throughout the day busloads of Americans continued to pour down the desert road to Alexandria. In the afternoon, on instructions, I gave my American colleague and other friendly Missions the warning that all traffic should be clear of the vicinity of the airfields at Cairo West and Denkheila (Alexandria) by sundown. At the request of the Americans, I telegraphed to London that an American convoy was passing down the road to Alexandria the same evening. As a result, British bombers, which had already taken off from Cyprus to bomb Cairo West airfield, were turned back to Cyprus. In the course of the day, members of the locally engaged staff and their families began to congregate in the Embassy compound and by nightfall the majority of the British staff were already inside, prepared to sleep, as best they might, on the floor of

their offices. At sunset the first bombs fell on the airfields round Cairo. We could clearly hear the
explosions and the night sky was lit up with flares and
fires. Raids continued throughout the night.

On 30 October we had started burning our papers.
We had no time to separate the confidential from the
rest: we burnt the lot, inside the chancery and outside
on the lawn, until we were inches deep in ash and had
showered the neighbourhood. At noon on 1 November
I was summoned to the Foreign Ministry by the Deputy
Foreign Minister and the Chief of Protocol who had
been dining with us only a week or two before, and
told that the Egyptians were breaking off relations. We
sent fifty-five members of the staff under police escort
by train to Alexandria, to catch a ship leaving on 1
November, having received assurances both before and
after the breach of relations, that the party would be
allowed to leave. The officials at Alexandria refused to
allow them to go, and they had to stay in a hotel until
they joined us on the way out. We remained anxious
about them until we had news, but were glad that we
had this many less people in the Embassy compound.

At the same time, exit permits were refused to all
British subjects. A few got away on ships passing
through the Canal. The airports were closed and there
was no ship leaving Alexandria during the time when
they could get exit permits. The journey by rail and
boat to the Sudan was not judged safe during the bombing. The massacre of 1919 in Upper Egypt was still in
people's minds. In any case, there was no time to
arrange a journey to the Sudan before exit permits were
stopped. The contractors' employees were in Egypt on
the British Government's business and the British
Government therefore had a special obligation to look
after them. They were in the most sensitive area. But we
could do nothing for them, since they were in private
employment and had no official status. They had the

warning of 30 October at 11 a.m. on that day. They
were arrested by the Egyptian police at 11.30 p.m. on 31
October. Two got away by road to the Libyan frontier.
The Egyptians clearly wanted to clear the Canal area of
British. The rest were taken at night without their
luggage to Cairo and interned there until their release
before Christmas. Virtually no members of the British
Community were able to act on the last warning.

Months before, I had agreed with the Foreign Office
that if diplomatic relations were broken off, the Swiss
should be asked to look after our interests. The Swiss
chargé d'affaires received his instructions on the
morning of 2 November. Fortunately, Monsieur Guy
de Keller and his American wife had been our closest
friends outside the Embassy. We had shared a tent in
the desert and had ridden together several times a week.
Together, we were now able to deal with the more
tiresome incidents of an uncomfortable situation with
complete understanding. At noon on 2 November, the
gates of the Embassy were closed by the Egyptians. An
armed guard was posted; my police escort became my
gaolers; no one was allowed in or out; our telephone
went dead and the electricity was cut off. The Egyptians
were obviously nervous that we might get up to tricks
with Nasser's political opponents and wished to cut our
communications with the outside world. Some visitors
had been locked in with us; some of the staff had been
locked out. It took us a whole day to get this sorted out.
It took two days to get back our electric power, after
our transmitters had been sealed by the Swiss. It took
three days to get a single telephone line open to the
Swiss Legation.

During the summer we had acquired against an
emergency army 'compo' packs sufficient to feed fifty
people for three days. We were a hundred inside the
Embassy and might be there for a long time. Our
servants were not allowed to go out and buy our food,

and, though very loyal to us, found they had to leave
us after a few days. We were told that we could not get
provisions from our normal suppliers owing to the
prohibitions in the 'Trading with the Enemy Act'
promulgated a day or two before, and it needed prolonged argument before the Egyptian officials could be
induced to admit that we must be fed and to allow the
Swiss to act as middlemen. On 2 November we had been
down to two biscuits, an apple and a cup of tea for
breakfast and we had had to supplement our servants'
food from our emergency store.

We were relieved in a moment of some anxiety by the
timely help arranged by the Swiss, of Mr A. R. Cutler,
my Australian colleague, himself interned a few days
later, a six foot five V.C., who arrived outside the gate
with ample supplies of fresh food, which the guards,
prudently in view of Mr Cutler's size and resolute
demeanour, allowed to be passed over the gate. We
were able after some days to buy blankets and
mattresses; we got permission for a doctor to come and
treat a bad case of blood poisoning; we even had visits
from the Anglican bishop and a Roman Catholic priest
on the one Sunday of our internment. Each of our
requirements had to be wrung out of the Egyptian
Ministries by the Swiss, but we observed no desire by
the Egyptian authorities to humiliate or tease us. The
Egyptian Departments were normally not very efficient
and had been thrown into some confusion by the events
of the last few days. Thanks to Swiss help, we suffered
no more than minor inconveniences.

The Swiss chargé fought a notable battle in defence
of our compound against the attempts of the Egyptian
Police to raid it and carry off our transmitters and spare
generator. He won, on condition that he personally
sealed all equipment capable of transmitting wireless
messages. He started one evening and sealed one room.
Next morning he returned to continue. The sealed door

was open. Alarm and despondency was registered. Our maintenance engineer had the face of a stained-glass angel, blue eyes, fair hair and all, the resourcefulness of a sailor and the fingers of a pickpocket. The door was resealed. The transmission room was sealed. The outer door was locked. 'But I have made myself a pass-key,' explained the engineer, 'and I can open any door in the office.' The spare generator room was sealed. 'I think,' said the engineer, 'I had better show you this,' and opened another room full of equipment. We sealed it. The engineer revealed another room, then his work-room. All were sealed. 'Of course,' said the candid engineer, 'I can make a transmitting set out of any receiving set in the house,' and went on to enlarge on what he could do with various bits and pieces. 'For Heaven's sake, that's enough,' said the exhausted chargé, 'don't tell me any more.' He was having a hard enough time reconciling his duties to the Egyptian Government with his natural inclination not to be unpleasant to us. He will never, I think, forget the disconcerting young engineer with his blue eyes and golden hair, opening his endless series of work-rooms, always with something more to seal.

We were a mixed crowd, reflecting the history of the British connection with Egypt. We had with us old soldiers who had married and retired in Egypt. We were of many national origins, Maltese, Cypriots and Levantines included. We had mothers with small children and grandmothers. We were determined to leave behind a smart Embassy, not a discarded refugee camp. Under the general supervision of Terence Garvey, the Head of Chancery, the military attaché, Brigadier Fraser, was in charge of administration, organising groups for cooking, cleaning and feeding. The oldest member of our senior staff, John Hamilton, was asked later what his task had been. He replied: 'I had an important task in prospect. If a crowd had tried to storm the gates, I was to parley with them. My actual task however was to clean the latrines.'

We saw little of the 'war'. I used to stand on the roof of the Embassy watching the firework display over Cairo West airfield. We saw only two Egyptian aircraft, Ilyushin bombers, fleeing South on the morning after the first attack, and an occasional Canberra doing photographic reconnaissance at 30,000 feet, while the Egyptian anti-aircraft shells burst harmlessly ten thousand feet or so below. We saw the French Thunderstreaks roar low over Cairo one afternoon, causing temporary alarm. Surely, we thought, this was not in the plans. We saw military transport continually bustling both ways past the Embassy. Tanks clattered up and down the corniche as soon as darkness fell. At the time of the landing, they seemed to be running for cover to the South. The sound of rifle practice by the 'National Liberation Army' formed a continuous background to our life, and the night was punctuated by bursts of unexplained small-arms fire.

We were concerned with the possible breakdown of public security. We calculated that we could hold out in the top floor of our new Chancery against a mob, even against attempts to burn us out, for about twenty-four hours, during which time, as I told de Keller, I should break his seals and wireless for British military help. Only once was the situation uncertain. On the evening of the day when the French jets had flown over, the street in front of the Chancery building was crammed with an excited crowd, shouting and shaking their fists, and the watchers on the roof thought they were coming over the wall. We decided that there should be no firing until I gave the order. However, the crowd eventually dispersed and otherwise all was peaceful. Not even extra police were posted. The passers-by showed no interest in us. I had been out in my conspicuous car with the flag flying on 1 November, and on foot on 2 November, just before we were shut up, and no one appeared even to notice me.

Some of us in Cairo were unhappy and puzzled. What sense did it make that the senior R.A.F. officer, who had lunched in my house so recently with his old pupil, the Commander of the Egyptian Air Force, should now be bombing that Air Force, which he had done so much to organise? Why did our action coincide with the Israeli attack? Why had we so suddenly abandoned our adherence to the tripartite declaration and declared that it did not apply to the Israeli attack on Egypt? Why had we warned the Israelis against attacking Jordan and not against attacking Egypt, even if we had a treaty with Jordan and not with Egypt? And why had this change of front come about so suddenly, when only a few days before, the British representative in the Security Council had been arguing vigorously in favour of Jordan and accusing the Israelis of aggression after only a minor frontier incident? Why did we take air action against the Egyptians, but not against the Israelis? Why did we not sit on the frontier instead of so far inside Egypt? We could only suspend judgement until we reached home.

Nor could we understand the course of events. Why did the Forces not land? Why these days of preliminary bombing? It never crossed our minds that anyone might believe that the bombing might in itself bring about Egyptian capitulation. On the contrary, everything possible was being done by our Forces to make the Egyptians realise that they would not get hurt. When we received the first telegram 'en clair' announcing the targets for the first night's attack, we believed that a mistake had been made and immediately telegraphed about it. Our Forces were behaving in a humane way; the Egyptians knew that when the R.A.F. told them their objectives in advance, they could trust their word and their ability to do what they said. It was all the better for Nasser. The Forces landed. We heard the wireless reports of the scene in the House of Commons. What was all this waving of order papers and excitement? Since when had Members of Parliament regarded a few units of the Egyptian army as a serious enemy? How could we treat our action, however well conducted, as a serious military operation? We had thought that there must be some explanation coming. We heard the broadcasts of the political leaders and were not reassured. Then we heard that the British and French Forces were going to stop short of Ismailia. Whatever our views about the attack, we all felt that to announce that we were going to occupy Port Said, Ismailia and Suez and then only to occupy Port Said, was all wrong.

On 2 November I had written that, politics apart, it was to me a miserable business. In spite of all the difficulties and disappointments, my wife and I had had a most happy life in Cairo. We had found friendly Egyptians of all classes. We had come to love the country, the view of the Pyramids on our desert rides to Sakkara, the jagged mountains rising out of the Red Sea desert, the turquoise Mediterranean Sea. Now, in three days, the impossible had happened. It did not seem to make sense. The house and office had been turned into a refugee camp; we were besieged with no lights or telephone and Cairo was lit up at night by red flares dropped by the R.A.F. For some days I had shrugged it all off, but on that day when the Egyptian household staff came to say good-bye, I was greatly affected and it was borne in on me that all that I had been trying to build was in ruins and the life that I had led no longer existed. I was not making, I wrote, a political judgement. It was a statement of fact. It was, I confess, difficult at that time not to come near to tears, not of self-pity, but of vexation and despair.

We received great encouragement from our friends

in the Diplomatic Corps outside. I heard of the Egyptian doctor who said: 'We don't like the French; but we don't really dislike the British. After all, who but the British would have done such a nasty thing in such a nice way?' One of the Swiss told us that he had seen a crowd round a restaurant and heard them saying 'Parachutist'. He had elbowed his way in. An obvious young Scandinavian tourist was sitting at a table, totally unaware of the interest which he was arousing, and of what was going on. He had hitch-hiked from Suez to Cairo. 'What a strange country,' he said. 'There seems to be nothing on the roads except military transport.'

A Swiss team arrived from the Sudan to take charge of British and French interests. They were told that we were all to be over the frontier in twenty-four hours, an absurd statement to which we paid no attention. At least, we knew that the Egyptian Government now wanted to get rid of us. We were not surprised. They may have feared that a provocative incident would be organised in order to give the British and French Forces on the Canal an excuse to attack Cairo, or that we might still get into touch with their opponents. In spite of our confinement, this would not have been difficult, if we had wanted it, judging by the commercial transactions which used to go on through the bars under the eyes of the Police. The airfields were out of commission. There were no ships in the ports. They would obviously not want to put us across the Lines into Port Said. For some time, it looked like Wadi Halfa. We were prepared to agree without enthusiasm. At last, the obvious route was chosen, the Libyan frontier. We wanted a car convoy. The Egyptians refused on the ground that protection would be difficult. For days we and the Swiss laboured to get an agreed list. I refused to move without the staffs of the consulates in Alexandria, Ismailia and Suez, the Service Attachés who had been stationed with the contractors and the fifty-

one Embassy employees held up in Alexandria.
Monsieur Koenig of the Swiss Mission fought stoutly
over the lists on our behalf. At last, it was arranged that
the special train for the French, the Australians and the
British should leave Cairo on the evening of Friday 10
November.

We prepared to leave that old Embassy on the Nile,
which had seen so much. Cromer had built it. He,
Kitchener, Wingate, Allenby, Lloyd had lived in it. Sir
Lee Stack, shot on the streets of Cairo, had been brought
into it to die; Allenby had set out from it with his
cavalry bodyguard to demand recompense for the
murder, stuffing into his pocket unopened the contrary
instructions received at that moment from London.
Wingate and Lloyd had been recalled from it, at odds
with the British Government. Sir Miles Lampson had
set off from it to surround the Abdin Palace with
British tanks. The records had been burnt there before,
when the Germans came near Alexandria. Winston
Churchill had enjoyed in it 'the princely hospitality of
Sir Miles Lampson', as he phrased it, and had learnt, as
he climbed its formidable staircase, of the death of Gott,
his chosen commander, at a moment of crisis. In
January 1952 one could have heard the cries of the
Cairo mob and seen the reflection of the fires at the
Turf Club and Shepheard's. Now, the Hilton hotel was
rising on the site of the Kasr ul Nil barracks. A high
block of flats and the new Shepheard's occupied the
river position to the North, which could have been
bought at one time by the British for a fraction of its
later value and which blocked out the cooling northern
breeze, thus giving rise to the saying that the British
Embassy never did know which way the wind was
blowing in Egypt. In imperial days the garden had
extended to the Nile. Now it was cut off from the river
by a busy corniche road. A new Chancery had been
built, too large for any future requirements, showing

how mistaken were the assessments of our future
position in Egypt. A new garden had been made, the
fountain decorated with dolphins specially chosen by
the Ministry of Works as non-political animals. The
winter was at hand; the Ekkiad shoot was due to start
in ten days. It had all gone up in smoke.

I was to be escorted to the station by the Swiss
Minister who had just managed to get back. Madame
de Keller and her small son were coming with us on
the train and sat with us in the library, from which the
portraits of Cromer, Kitchener and Allenby looked at
us with disapproval. Monsieur de Keller was at the gate,
arguing with the Egyptians about the order in which
we should set out for the station. At last, in the late
evening, all was ready. Madame de Keller and her little
son left the room first. I followed with the Swiss
Minister, put out the lights in the study and the hall,
turned the large brass key in the lock and left that great
building shuttered, locked and dark. We walked to the
gate. There was a crash of glass from the Embassy. We
rushed back and opened the door. Out came Madame
de Keller, holding her wrist, saying: 'I am bleeding.'
Unknown to us, she had been to the bathroom with her
son. When the lights went out, she had groped her way
to the door. It was pitch black. She called and knocked.
No one heard. Fearing that the cars might leave without
her absence being noticed, she pulled hard on the door
handle. It came off. She broke the glass panel to attract
attention. A piece of glass flew back and cut the artery
on her wrist. A tourniquet was quickly made and she
was taken to hospital. And so I left the Embassy with
the front porch covered with glass and blood.

The journey to the frontier was without incident. No
one showed any interest in us. At Alexandria I stood on
the platform, ignoring flags and whistles until the last
of our staff had been allowed on the train. We passed
Alamein. Less than three weeks before we had been

there for the Alamein Day Service, with the Egyptian General commanding in Alexandria representing the Egyptian Government and Egyptian bugles sounding the Last Post. Our train was full of Police, in uniform and in plain clothes, including my old guard, as friendly as ever. One said : 'We had to defend our country; but we must admit it is in an awful mess.' A plain clothes detective asked my Counsellor, Mr Evans, whether he knew Mr Evans. Evans identified himself. 'That is very interesting,' said the policeman. 'I have been shadowing you for the last three months.' Men of the Cyrenaica Defence Force came over the frontier to escort us from the train into Libya, being compelled by the Egyptians to leave their weapons behind. I crossed the frontier last. I felt no sense of relief, only that I was going the wrong way, leaving behind my job, my house, my friends, and, most important, the British Community in trouble. Next day I left Tobruk for London. My Naval Attaché remarked gloomily: 'I have never travelled over this bit of the map from here to Malta, without the vehicle in which I was travelling bursting into flames.' However, Providence decided that we had had enough and we arrived in London on the evening of 13 November. The final act had taken only just over two weeks.

13

So ended my time in Egypt. Passing through Libya, I had heard that the British Forces there had been told some days before the end of October to have their security tightened up by the end of the month. This induced speculation. On my return, I did not conceal that I had had no previous warning that the British Government were sending the Egyptians an ultimatum. How could I have had such a warning, since the Prime Minister had told Parliament on 30 October that the decision had been taken only that morning as a consequence of the Israeli attack on 29 October? Privately, I was heartily glad that I had not known more. I found that if I had been ignored, so had practically the whole of the Foreign Office and that a crisis of confidence had been created between Ministers and officials. It was not surprising that even as late as 30 October we in Cairo had not expected a British and French attack. Nasser told Mr Nutting later that he had estimated the chances of an Anglo-French direct attack on the Canal at 40%, an attack following an Israeli attack at nil. If we had been asked this in Cairo, we should have given about the same reply. In Cairo it was inconceivable that we should intervene as a result of an Israeli attack except to stop the Israelis through

the United Nations or on the basis of the tripartite
declaration. I was satisfied that we could have done no
more for the British Community and was not concerned
for their personal safety, though distressed that we had
to leave them behind. I was grateful to the leaders of
the Community who supported me before and after the
event, and to *The Times* which published a turnover
article on the British Community in Egypt, and
effectively dispelled criticism of the Embassy.

The Community showed courage and restraint.
Many were expelled, losing their livelihood and posses-
sions with little prospect of adequate compensation.
Some were for a time imprisoned, including one very
old lady who had come to Egypt before the bombardment of Alexandria in 1882 and who had devoted her
life to serving the Egyptian people. Many had come to
regard Egypt as their country. On my return I worked
for some months to help their resettlement and remedy
their legitimate grievances. I was disappointed that I
could not achieve more; but much of what I had asked
for, was afterwards conceded under the pressure in the
House of Lords led by Lord Killearn.

As a civil servant, I was not involved in the
controversy which raged so fiercely and so long and
which for a time split the country. Whatever might be
said about the morality of our action, we had started
something which had failed and could surely never have
been successful against the international pressures. Sir
Winston Churchill had been right when he said that he
would not have done it without the Americans. In
Cairo we had deplored that the British Forces did not
go as far as Suez since it had been said they would; but
we had never believed that if they had, it would have
made any difference to the outcome.

We had not believed the stories that preparations had
been made for Russian participation in an Egyptian
attack on the Israelis. Nor, on the other hand, did we

take the Russian threats seriously. The Russians were trying to divert attention from Hungary, to cause us as much trouble as possible and to increase their influence in Egypt and the rest of the Arab world by giving Egypt all possible support; but they were not likely to get too deeply involved themselves, nor to risk causing the Americans to swing over to the other side. They needed to do no more than pretend that their threats had been the decisive reason for our withdrawal. With the Americans and nearly every other country in the United Nations against us, the pressure was strong enough to get us out. It was argued that the British Government had only the choice between action or passivity in the face of danger and that their action was necessary in order to stop a 'forest fire' in the Middle East. But a forest fire at that moment might have done some good, and if the object was to take Nasser down a peg, the best way of doing it would have been to let the Israelis defeat the Egyptians on their own.

In 1882 the bombardment of Alexandria and the British occupation of Egypt had divided British opinion on the same lines. John Bright had declared the British action to be 'a manifest violation of international and moral law', while Lord Randolph Churchill had accused Mr Gladstone of an act of criminal aggression against Egypt and demanded that he should be thrown out of Egypt bag and baggage;[1] but we had stayed there for seventy-three years. On this occasion, the basic cause of our failure was that what we could do in 1882, we could not do in 1956. We no longer had the same power in the world and miscalculated the forces which could be brought to bear on the situation. It was an expensive aberration. I recalled how Nasser had said to me earlier: 'You are suddenly acting in the sort of way we do.' We lost much by it in prestige and position in the

[1] Quoted by Philip Magnus, *Gladstone* (1954).

Middle East, but I thought at the time that this could be overstated. Nasser had taken a knock too. Even before Suez we no longer had the dominant position of the past. There was not so much to lose as some people imagined. As a result of the Suez affair we did not wholly lose such influence as we had had, at least outside Egypt. Twice after this, we intervened successfully in the Middle East in the old way, once with the Americans in 1958 in the Lebanon and Jordan, and again in 1961 in Kuwait, when Arab interests were divided. On both occasions we were invited in by the legitimate Government. But Suez made us begin to realise what the Arab world now was. It projected us into the mid-twentieth century.

There was an epilogue. In 1967, in the face of some provocation, the Israelis attacked again. The shadow of 1956 helped to obtain belief for the groundless accusations that we were actively on the Israeli side. The Israelis sat on the Canal and the Egyptians again sank blockships in it. So the statement of British Ministers on 5 October 1956 that we were intervening to keep the Canal open, proved in retrospect to be truer than anyone in the Middle East had believed at the time it was made.

BAGHDAD, 1958-61

Kiss the hands that you cannot cut off.
Middle Eastern proverb

*Si ton ennemi t'outrage, va t'asseoir devant
ta porte: tu verras passer son cadavre.*
Arab proverb, quoted by Malraux

*J'avais répondu autrefois à Saint-Exupéry,
qui me demandait ce que je pensais de courage,
qu'il me semblait une conséquence curieuse
et banale du sentiment d'invulnerabilité.*
Malraux, *Anti-Mémoires*

AFTER the first world war, the British brought to Baghdad the Hashemites, the family of King Hussein of the Hejaz, the leading figure in the Arab revolt against the Turks. The Emir Feisal reigned for a brief period in Damascus, but was expelled by the French when they received the mandate over Syria. The British then put him on the throne of Iraq, which had been placed under British mandate in 1920 by the San Remo conference. In 1932 the mandate was terminated and Iraq became independent. The new Anglo-Iraqi treaty, which was to run for twenty-five years, maintained the close British connection with Iraq and became increasingly a subject of political contention, as Arab nationalism grew stronger. The revolts of Baqr Sidki in 1936 and Rashid Ali in 1941 made no permanent imprint and failed to overthrow the Hashemite rule. By 1948 the Iraqi régime realised the necessity of revising the treaty in conformity with current political opinion and, as a consequence, a new Anglo-Iraqi treaty was signed at Portsmouth. While the Iraqi leaders dallied in Europe, the Baghdad street erupted and the new treaty was buried. The Hashemite throne still survived.

So the old treaty continued in force until the Baghdad

*Pact was signed in February 1955 by Turkey and Iraq
and gave a new opportunity for revision of the treaty
under cover of the new alliance. In April 1955 Britain
adhered to the Pact. At the same time the old treaty was
abrogated and a bilateral agreement was signed between
Britain and Iraq, under which Britain was to evacuate
the British bases in Iraq, leaving only R.A.F. staging
posts and a military mission, but continuing to
guarantee the defence of Iraq. The new arrangements
were put into effect and survived with some difficulty
the effects in Iraq of the Anglo-French action against
Suez, largely through the efforts of Nuri Said who
remained the most influential and controversial
politician in Iraq and a steadfast friend of Britain, a
position which was not so firm a basis for policy as it
had been thirty-five years before.*

*Revolution is endemic in Iraq and the forces oppos-
ing the régime of Nuri and his friends and the British
connection gained strength from the success of Nasser
at Suez, the growth of his prestige as leader of Arab
nationalism and the propaganda of Cairo radio which
attacked the Baghdad Pact and the Iraqi Government.
The last major act of policy of the Hashemite régime
was to form the Hashemite Union of Iraq and Jordan.
This device, which had not yet acquired a serious
content, disappeared without trace on the first day of
the 1958 revolution.*

*While Iraq was in revolution, Lebanon was in
turmoil and Jordan became dangerously unstable.
American Forces landed in the Lebanon and British
Forces in Jordan at the request of the two Governments
and the situation in both was soon restored. The Iraqi
revolution continued on its way without outside
intervention.*

inspiration, but the conspirators must have been inspired by the Egyptian example and had the advantage of several years of attack by the Egyptian Radio on Nuri Said and the Hashemite régime. At the beginning it was Abdul Nasser's photograph which replaced the King's. A few politicians from the opposition were privy to the plot, but it was essentially an Army coup. There had been several plans which had not been carried out and, inevitably in Iraq, rumours of a coup in preparation. It was widely believed in Iraq that the Chief of Staff had been told of the plot and had been given the names of the plotters, but that he had refused to believe the information. Qasim had been a favourite of the Crown Prince and Nuri. At the time of the revolution, he was commanding a brigade of the third division at Baquba, about forty miles East of Baghdad, towards the Iranian frontier. Major General Daghestani, who commanded the division, told me later that he had had no suspicion of Qasim's loyalty.

The conspirators' opportunity came when Nuri Said ordered the third division to move to Jordan. To reach the desert road to the West, they had to pass through Baghdad. It had been a rule that troops from outside Baghdad should not move through Baghdad with their ammunition, but this rule was broken. The conspirators had luck on their side, since they were to move on the night before the King and Crown Prince were due to leave for Ankara in the early morning. Abdul Salam Arif conducted the attack in Baghdad, while Qasim was still up the road at Baquba. At about 6 a.m. on 14 July 1958, Arif's troops captured the Baghdad radio station and attacked the palace with tanks and armoured cars. There was a short battle with the King's body-guard, but the attackers were too strong for them. The Crown Prince and the King came out into the garden, presumably to parley with the rebels, and were shot there. The ladies of the palace were shot soon after.

Nuri Said temporarily escaped from his house, dressed as a woman, but was shot the next day. The bodies of the Crown Prince and Nuri Said were dragged through the streets. The story that the conspirators intended to spare the King is doubtful. He was popular and, unlike Farouk, could in exile have become the focus of counter-revolution.

Early on the same day, the crowd, urged on by the revolutionary radio, pulled down the statues of Feisal I and General Maude, the liberator of Iraq from Turkish rule, and attacked the British Embassy. A member of the Ambassador's personal staff was killed by a stray bullet. The Ambassador, his wife and those of the staff who had arrived to work, were forced to take refuge in the Registry where they started to burn the secret papers. They were beseiged by the crowd and were told to come out or be burnt out. They had no choice. As they came out, the crowd snatched their watches and trinkets, but they were otherwise unharmed. A detachment of Iraqi soldiers belatedly appeared and marshalled the Embassy staff on the lawn, pointing their weapons at them and making no effort to stop the crowd, who were looting and setting fire to the Ambassador's house. Boats were brought up the river to take away the heavier pieces of furniture and everything which could be moved or torn away was taken, until the flames drove off the looters. The temperature was around 114° in the shade. The party were kept in the open throughout the day and were only released in the evening. A book on Chinese jades was found by a Dutch engineer three years later on a rubbish heap a hundred miles south of Baghdad. Nothing else of the looted property was seen again.

There was another distressing incident on that day. The Police, looking for the Jordanian members of the Council of the Hashemite Union, picked up from the newly opened Baghdad Hotel two Jordanians and, for good measure, one German and two American business-men and drove them off in a lorry to the Ministry of Defence. Near the Ministry they were stopped by a hostile crowd, which apparently thought that they had identified one of the politicians of the old régime on the lorry. The crowd pulled the prisoners off the lorry. One Jordanian escaped into the Ministry. The remaining prisoners were lynched and their bodies dragged along the street. The bodies of the murdered men and women, Iraqi and foreign, were buried in a secret grave. We were never told where it was.

The bulk of the Army hesitated. General Iskander Mirza, when President of Pakistan, told me that he thought intervention from outside in the first twenty-four hours would have overthrown the new régime, but after that it was too late. But there was no chance of it at any time. Jordan was internally far too weak and the experience of Suez hardly encouraged our intervention. It would have been a foolish and unprofitable action. No Government established by British force could have lasted. The old order could not be brought back. Most of the senior Iraqi officers quickly found it wise to conform. The leading politicians and soldiers most closely identified with the old régime were arrested. All other politicians from the Communists to the Nasserists supported the revolution. General Dag-hestani, Qasim's old superior officer, was brought into Baghdad in a jeep, barely escaping with his life from a hostile crowd shouting that he must be 'dragged'. Qasim met him in the Ministry of Defence and told him that he need not worry; he would be released in a few days. Daghestani replied that the new Government had set up a revolutionary court to try members of the old régime. He had done nothing of which he was ashamed, nothing against his country's interests. They should try him too. He was a brave man.

Qasim soon began to find out that those who had

been opposed to the old régime and had therefore
supported the revolution, were not likely to be any
more amenable to the new régime, and that those who
had made the revolution would not stick together for
long. During the first five months of the revolution he
survived two serious challenges to his power. He
quickly quarrelled with Abdul Salam Arif, his chief
companion in the plot. Arif stumped the country with
demagogic speeches and soon revealed himself as intent
on bringing Iraq into Nasser's orbit. Qasim dealt with
Arif easily. He exiled him by appointing him
Ambassador in Germany. Arif did not join his post, but
stayed in Switzerland. Qasim called him back, staged a
scene in which he alleged, almost certainly falsely, that
Arif had tried to kill him, having his hand already on
his pistol, arrested him and had him sentenced to death.
The trial was held in camera and the evidence and
verdict were suppressed until Qasim considered his
position safe enough to allow their publication.

Soon after, Rashid Ali Gailani, the old rebel of 1941,
under sentence of death until the revolution, who had
been called back by Qasim, imprudently indulged in a
half-baked plot, ignoring his friends' warnings. The
conspirators were indiscreet and the plot was widely
known about inside and outside Iraq. Qasim had no
difficulty in suppressing it. He arrested Rashid Ali
Gailani and sentenced him to death. There was a back-
lash on us. Cairo radio broadcast that we had warned
Qasim and for many months assiduously propagated
the view that we were in alliance with the Communists
in Iraq to support Qasim against Nasser, a view which
never completely died out in Iraq, however hostile
Qasim became to us, and which even found some
credence in Europe, being summed up some months
later in an article in *Der Spiegel* under the title 'Der
feind steht am Nil'. My predecessor, Sir Michael
Wright, had met the challenge of the revolution with

fortitude and common-sense. He rightly felt that his own close personal association with the old régime made it undesirable for him to stay in Iraq and I had been appointed to succeed him. At this point, in early December 1958, I came in.

in central and southern Iraq were confiscated long
before the Government were in a position to provide
the services formerly provided by the landlord, and
there was no rational system of land distribution to fit
the irrigation system. Glib statements about the provision of services by co-operatives were meaningless
in a country of uneducated peasants in which there were
few co-operatives and no experienced men to develop
them. Three years after the revolution the only result
of the Government's co-operative policy was the disappearance of the only co-operative societies in
existence before the revolution.

There were other complications. The Department in
charge of Land Reform was in the hands of Communists
who were determined to secure Communist control of
the countryside, in many areas of which the officials
were soon powerless. Terrorisation and murder were
common. Squatters invaded the old estates. The landlords could not even cultivate the land left to them by
the law. In the first two years after the revolution crops
were reduced by a half and the land affected by the law
was in large part left uncultivated. The Government
leased some land to the peasants and gave them seed.
The seed was mostly eaten or sold and the lease money
was not paid. Crops were sown only by the small landowners not touched by land reform and on the estates
in the North, where the land reform officials dared not
touch the still powerful Kurdish and Arab sheikhs. At
one time the Government begged the old landowners
to resume possession of their estates temporarily until
the new distribution could be carried out, but they
could not have done so even if they had been willing.
Large imports of wheat were necessary. This suited the
Government well enough. Instead of buying local wheat
at a subsidised rate and selling it at a loss, they could
make a profit on cheaper Australian wheat, foreign
exchange from the oil royalties being plentiful. While

the peasants' associations began to take the place of the officials, the village schools were getting into Communist hands. We were out shooting. An aircraft appeared overhead. 'Mig,' said a small boy. It seemed that Communism was getting well dug in.

In the towns the Communists gained control of the Trades Unions, which had been formed immediately after the revolution. They disrupted work wherever they could. They had the workers and students out on the streets two or three times a week. They forced the Government to give bonuses all round. The cost of labour substantially increased; output for a time was halved. They secured control in some Ministries and in the university. Communist front organisations were formed and were patronised by Qasim, who made no effort to get the workers back to work and declared that all the students who had failed in their examinations should be deemed to have passed. Little good it did them. They were known to their fellow students as the 'creepers' and many of them found it better to try again and pass on their own merits.

The Communists gained control of virtually all publicity media. The Government radio and television plugged the Communist line. The Press was overwhelmingly Communist in tone. The Communists created the Popular Resistance Force, a para-military organisation which took over control of the streets at night and which was presumably designed as a private army to help them to power. The Security Forces were undermined. The Army and Police Officers who in the past had used force to quell civil disorder, were being tried for arbitrary action against 'the people'. No Police or Army Officer would now stick his neck out to restore order in the streets while the Communist mob was shouting for Qasim. The morale of the Army was disintegrating. Many N.C.O.s and soldiers and some officers were now Communists, a few from conviction, more from opportunism, and nationalist officers were lying low. In December 1958 the Communists were able to besiege the Garrison Commander of Basra in his headquarters and open encouragement of soldiers by the People's Court to attack 'disloyal' officers was followed by the murder in Basra of a Colonel by men of his unit. The Police were discredited and powerless in the face of the Popular Resistance Force.

British and other foreigners working in Iraq came under some pressure, apart from the difficulties of carrying on business without increasing losses in the general chaos and lack of labour discipline. There was no general drive against them, but at any moment a man might receive an order to leave in a few days and there were moments of danger to individuals caught up in this fantasy which passed for Government. One morning my telephone rang. An English voice said : 'I am being besieged in my office by my workers who threaten to drag me through the streets. Send help at once.' He was rescued. At the Basra Power Station then being built, a German workman during the lunch break was seeing how high he could kick up the wall and accidentally tore a photograph of Qasim greeting a mob in the Baghdad streets. A Communist worker passing by saw it through the window. Immediately the room in which the foreigners were having lunch, was surrounded by a screaming crowd carrying ropes and threatening to hang the man on the nearest post. A Pakistani girl clerk at the British Council office was accused falsely of tearing up a photograph of Qasim, a frequent accusation at this time, and was ordered to leave the country. The real reason for the order was simple. In the street in which she lived, an old woman was carrying on a thriving trade supplying girls and boys to officers in the army. She was doing so well that she wished to extend her business and needed the house which the girl occupied.

British bank employees were at risk from subordinates who disliked their orders. We had to protest
and argue continually to get orders of expulsion
reversed. Sometimes, official action was merely funny.
An employee of a British bank asked the C.I.D. why
they were following him. The explanation was un-
expected. In Arabic the middle name counts. His
middle name was Macmillan. They thought he must
be the Prime Minister's son and therefore a British
agent. But the British Community remained relatively
unmolested in their offices and clubs and during the
first three years of the revolution our trade continued
to flow at a rate not appreciably lower than before the
revolution. There was no obvious discrimination
against the British.

The notorious Colonel Medhawi, a cousin of Qasim,
presided over the People's Court. He had been an un-
distinguished officer in a supply unit. He was violent
and unprincipled, abusive and shameless, and was determined to have all the leaders of the old régime
executed. It was a political court, a staged show, interrupted at frequent intervals by a claque chanting praises
for Qasim and Medhawi and cursing the accused in the
dock. Medhawi made no pretence of administering
justice. He delivered rabid political diatribes against
the British and the Americans, the old régime and later,
when the political climate changed, also against Nasser
and the United Arab Republic, the new name for
Egypt. Every evening the People's Court was the staple
entertainment in the Baghdad coffee houses on the
television recently installed by a British firm. On 31
December 1958, at a New Year's Eve party at the Railway Club, Medhawi shouted to the guests at midnight:
'I have a New Year present for you, twelve executions.'
Qasim used him as his mouthpiece for political propaganda, letting him go beyond the limits which Qasim
thought it prudent to observe himself. Anthony Nutting

published an interview with Qasim in which he attacked Colonel Medhawi. The next day Medhawi in court referred to 'this Natin', which means in Arabic the stink of a decomposing corpse, being careful, however, to explain that he was referring to Nutting's politics and not to his person. His enemies were delighted when he tripped up by extolling an Egyptian woman witness as a lioness, but using a word which meant prostitute in Egyptian Arabic. This fat, ugly, crazy man became for a brief period the hero of the Iraqi mob.

The principal figures of the old régime were duly condemned to death; soldiers such as Rafiq Arif, the former Chief of Staff and Ghazi Daghestani who had refused Qasim's clemency, and politicians such as Towfiq Suweidi, many times Prime Minister, known as the red fox, Fadhil Jamali, a familiar figure in the United Nations, noted for his anti-zionist and anti-Nasserist views, Said Qazzaz, the Kurdish former Minister of the Interior, hated and feared by the Communists and respected by everyone else. The accused stood up to the insults and screaming abuse of the Court with dignity and steadfastness, among the most staunch and unyielding being Said Qazzaz who was to fall a victim to Qasim in 1959. Qasim let Medhawi have his head in court, but not his way outside it. The Communists continually pressed for executions and Medhawi time and again hinted that they were not far off; but the cautious Qasim held his hand.

After the revolution a Government of civilians and soldiers had been formed from all parties other than the old régime. The leaders of the Communist party were close to Qasim, but not represented in the Government. The other parties, Ba'athists, Nasserists, moderate Nationalists, national democrats, were all represented. Within this structure the real power lay with Qasim and his military staff, down to the man who had been Nuri Said's A.D.C. and who boasted, without truth,

that he had murdered his former master. Qasim's headquarters was the Ministry of Defence, in which he was
protected by an infantry battalion which formed his
Praetorian guard. Not surprisingly, by December 1958
the heterogeneous collection of Ministers showed signs
of breaking apart. The Nationalist Foreign Minister,
plucking nervously at his lower lip, was obviously
acutely unhappy. The representative of the old Independence party, Nuri's old enemy, admitted at my
first call to having stayed at home in pique for the last
two months. The Ba'athist, at a Government reception,
asked me whether I did not think that Nasser was the
only possible saviour of the Arab world. The Kurdish
Minister told me that he was quite sure that Qasim was
a Communist. No other explanation could account for
his actions since the revolution.

By February 1959 the so-called National Front broke
up. The right-wing Ba'athists and Nationalists resigned,
unwilling to be associated any longer with the growing
Communist influence. They were followed by two of
the more prominent revolutionary officers, one of them
in disgust at Colonel Medhawi's behaviour. A member
of the National Democratic party was appointed Minister of Guidance. On his first day of office he suspended
the Communist Party newspapers for ten days. Qasim
reversed the order and he resigned. Qasim declared that
he would never suspend any newspaper (a declaration
which was later conveniently forgotten); but no newspaper could continue publication unless it took the
Government line, heavily weighted in favour of the
Communists. Qasim was now supported only by the
left, one or two from the left-centre and a few officers,
and was taking the Government more and more into
his own hands. The Ministers soon lost any real power.

At this point the Nationalists, supported by the
Egyptians, decided to act. We heard of open disaffection
in the higher Army ranks in Mosul and of a coming

coup. We even heard the date. So doubtless did Qasim, though not from us. We kept right out of Iraq's internal affairs. The conspiracy was to have broken simultaneously in Mosul and in Baghdad and perhaps in other centres also. It went off at half-cock. A new Government was proclaimed in Mosul and a rebel radio started to broadcast from there, taking the line that Qasim had distorted the true aims of the revolution. In Baghdad nothing happened. The conspirators at the Ministry of Defence took fright and failed to act.

A few days before the revolt Qasim had allowed or more probably instigated a large contingent of Communist sympathisers to go from Baghdad to Mosul, which was a nationalist stronghold, to take part in a demonstration in favour of the régime. This must have seemed to the conspirators to have foreshadowed official action against nationalists in Mosul and may have caused them to advance the date of the revolt, which occurred a few days before the date originally planned. One story current at the time was that Qasim had deliberately brought on the revolt before they were ready, by playing on the Baghdad radio the tune which he had learnt was to be the signal for the outbreak. In any case, the conspirators were ineffective. They succeeded in getting control of Mosul for a time and in arresting the Communist leaders there. One aircraft dropped a small bomb on military installations near Baghdad. Their radio would not work; so a posse of thugs descended on the Mosul Petroleum Company's headquarters and took away a British radio technician at the point of a pistol to mend it. He did the least he could, which was to point to a loose lead. In the room was an officer in Syrian uniform, and the case in which the transmitter had been packed, had Syrian markings. The authorities of the United Arab Republic did not seem to take any care to disguise their part in supporting the rebels.

Qasim acted promptly and decisively. The Iraqi Air Force, which was commanded by a known Communist, attacked the rebel headquarters with rocket-firing aircraft. The leader of the revolt was wounded and then shot by one of his own men, who saw that the game was up. Government Forces went into Mosul; the leading conspirators were arrested and the revolt was over. This gave the Communists their chance. In Mosul there were five days of anarchy, during which they looted, burnt and murdered their enemies, including many members of the leading families of the town. With the connivance of the authorities they established political courts to pronounce formal condemnation on their victims, whom they shot in the back in the streets or by a well outside Mosul which was to become notorious throughout Iraq. They did not foresee the vengeance which would descend on them when the tide turned.

In Baghdad the Communists demonstrated continuously, filling the streets with immense processions demanding the execution of traitors and praising Qasim. They now thought they had Qasim completely in their pocket. The Popular Resistance Force was well to the fore in Mosul, Baghdad and other towns. The propaganda organs screamed against Nasser and the imperialists. The name of Nasser, given to streets after the revolution, was removed. Photographs of his head were stuck on to photographs of striptease girls or donkeys in a sort of game of heads, bodies and legs, and were displayed on the principal shopping arcades. The Ambassador of the United Arab Republic was in Cairo at the time. Every possible restraint was put on his Embassy short of a breach of relations, which Qasim clearly wanted to avoid for political reasons. Seven members of the diplomatic staff were declared 'persona non grata' and the chargé d'affaires was put under strict surveillance. At this moment the Embassy celebrated one of their national days. They had invited a number of Ba'athist students who congregated in the garden while the Communist students collected outside, molested the guests, tried to invade the premises and even tried to set fire to the house. Official intervention was deliberately ineffective. The Egyptian-Iraqi honeymoon had lasted less than a year.

Qasim now opened a campaign to suppress the Nationalists. Over two hundred army officers were summarily retired. Many officers and civilians were imprisoned, some were undoubtedly maltreated. Among the prisoners were the Generals commanding the second division, Tabaqchali, and the third division, Ukhaili, who had just been appointed Ambassador in Teheran. We attended a party for Ukhaili in the house of the Iranian military attaché, who provided a conjuror. But the most effective trick had been performed before the party had begun. The principal guest had disappeared. He had visited Qasim in the Ministry of Defence to say farewell. Qasim had been very agreeable and told him not to hurry away. He went downstairs and was arrested at the door. One of the worst Communist cells was in the Railways Department, where, as was afterwards revealed, non-Communists were tortured. Sometime later, a senior Iraqi official told a member of my staff that he considered himself fortunate in having been dismissed from the Railways Department after the revolution. 'Otherwise,' he said, 'I should have found myself in that little room, and my eyes would have bulged out as the handkerchief was tightened round my neck.'

Many civil officials were dismissed. Some Nationalists went underground. Others escaped to Cairo and started broadcasting for Nasser. The Iraqi Ambassador in Cairo changed sides and resigned his post. The Communists stepped up their pressure in the towns and countryside. The Soviet Ambassador was everywhere acclaimed and fêted by the régime and the crowd. An agreement for economic and technical aid was signed with the Soviet Government, covering the building of factories and broadcasting stations, irrigation and mineral surveys and provision of a nuclear reactor. Soviet engineers and doctors moved in. Most of the British technicians were expelled. People began to believe that Qasim was a Communist and that the Communists would soon be in control.

3

Soon after the revolution Qasim had made an agreement with the Russians for the supply of arms, aircraft and miscellaneous military equipment. Obviously he was not going to continue to rely on British supplies and he was right in supposing that we should not have agreed to supply arms in the first few months after the revolution. However, in January 1959 he asked me for tanks, bombers, and heavy and anti-aircraft guns. Either he did not want to be wholly dependent for his arms on the Russians or he wanted to test our political attitude. There were reasons in favour of our agreeing. We did not want him to rely solely on the Russians. We could not refuse to sell him arms and hope to do business with him. We had interests to protect. On the other hand, it would be said that we had no business to be supplying arms to a man who had murdered our friends and appeared to be going Communist. Our allies in CENTO might object that we were giving preference to our enemies over our friends. Nasser might think it a renewed sign of our hostility to him. Israel would protest. For months the British Government shirked the issue, while the Communists in Iraq, as a result of the Mosul revolt, grew stronger.

We had to decide our attitude to Qasim and make an

assessment of probable developments in Iraq. I had
heard the view expressed that a take-over by Nasser in
Iraq was more to be feared than a take-over by the
Communists. For we knew how to deal with the Com-
unists and a Communist success in Iraq would have the
advantage of frightening the rest of the Arab world off
Communism. I did not subscribe to this view. I agreed
with an Iraqi friend from the old régime who had no
cause to love Nasser. He said to me that the Communist
threat was much the greater danger. For once the Communists were in, they could never be got out again,
whereas in Arab politics nothing was permanent. Others
expressed the view that Qasim was not a Communist
and that we should therefore support him. We in
Baghdad did not go as far as that. We did not know
whether Qasim was a Communist or not. He was more
probably a 'Qasimist', intent only on keeping power
and would not want anyone else to dominate him. Our
policy should be neither to support nor to oppose him,
but to do business with him so long as he remained in
power, if we could. The Americans at this time referred
to 1959 as the year of the bear in Iraq. We did not discount the dangers, but considered that Iraqi Nationalism was still the strongest force in the country and that
the Communists, whatever their apparent gains, would
not be able finally to take over power.

I recommended that we should agree to Qasim's
request and was summoned to London to discuss it.
Doubts were raised; gloomy forecasts were made of
hostile reactions by Parliament, our allies, Nasser. Mr
Selwyn Lloyd was direct and courageous. The Government decided to ignore the possible reactions and to do
what they thought right. The Cabinet agreed. It would
take at least a year to supply new tanks and aircraft
and we could always draw back if things went very badly
in Iraq. I made no predictions and promised no favourable results. Reactions to the decision were much more

favourable than had been feared. Nasser said that he understood our decision. Our Arab friends and CENTO allies agreed that it was a sensible policy. The Iranian Foreign Minister said to Mr Selwyn Lloyd: 'If a man is in a room with two windows and you shut one, he will look out of the other.'

I told Qasim, saying that the offer had no strings attached to it. However, he would understand that the basis of our relationship was that Iraq was not a Communist State. Many people thought that it already was one. The Communists were already saying that he was in their control. He replied that this was not true and accepted the offer. He got the political advantage of the advertisement that the British were prepared to deal with him. We got the advantage that he would not feel wholly dependent on the Russians. The negotiations were long. The Russians had the advantage of supplying at cut rates. The Communist Commander of the Air Force managed to block the sale of Canberras. In the end, Qasim took only spares and ammunition for the British arms which he already had. This suited us well enough politically. Qasim could not say that we had forced him to get all his arms from the Russians. We did not have to supply arms to a Government which was basically hostile to the West.

In his later speeches Qasim used to boast that he had destroyed the British bases at Habbaniya and Shaiba and expelled the imperialist Forces from the country. This was far from the truth. The British bases had been given up in 1955 as part of the revision of the Anglo-Iraqi treaty which accompanied the Baghdad Pact. All that was left at the revolution was an R.A.F. staging post and technicians helping to train the Iraqi Forces. Qasim had cut off all practical co-operation with the Baghdad Pact, but for many months Iraq remained formally a member of it. This was typical of Qasim's caution. He was still afraid of the reactions to a formal break. We did not bring the matter to a head. We still wanted to find out whether our staging rights could be continued.

One Sunday in the spring of 1959 Qasim told me that he agreed to staging rights for the R.A.F., provided that the Iraqi Air Force were in charge. I asked for instructions. I had recommended to London that the remaining R.A.F. personnel should leave Iraq. They were doing no good by staying. Their arms were locked up. They could not defend themselves against attack. They were now only a liability. On the Tuesday, two days after I had seen Qasim, he announced that Iraq had left the Baghdad Pact and that the special bilateral arrangement under which a British staging post remained, was therefore also abrogated. On the next Sunday I saw him again. I said that we had no objection to his leaving the Pact nor to the abrogation of the Special Agreement. This of course meant that British troops would now leave the country. We had been going to take them out anyway. We agreed to the proposal on staging which he had made on the previous Sunday. He replied that he had made that proposal before they had left the Baghdad Pact. There was now a completely new situation and the matter must be considered afresh. I replied that his proposal had therefore been valid for exactly two days. For once he appeared confused. This was typical of Qasim's trickery and was final proof, if we still needed any, that he was not to be trusted. About a year later I heard at second-hand from the Ministry of Defence that Qasim had said: 'I like Mr Trevelyan. He is a nice man. I tell him fantastic stories and he believes them all.' To this my answer was that he never told me anything definite enough to believe or disbelieve. His cunning over-reached itself. We had no illusions about him.

The arrangements for the evacuation of the R.A.F. men went smoothly. The Iraqis wanted them out. We wanted to get them out. At this time the Iraqi Security Department was not yet equipped with enough machines to record telephone conversations. One day during the 'Id' holidays we tried to telephone to Habbaniya. The exchange answered : 'Very sorry; you can't telephone to Habbaniya today; the listener is on holiday.' The Security Department was still in the bronze age. The last British troops left from Basra. I was heartily glad that we had got them out without incident.

The Security Police were moderately active against the British. No one could come to the Embassy without being questioned, and our visitors were sometimes arrested before they got inside or when they left. Craftsmen visiting staff houses were arrested in the middle of their job. The Military Attaché and the Arabic-speaking Counsellor were followed by the C.I.D. in cars or on motor-cycles. Telephone tapping became more efficient, though if you had two consecutive calls from the Baghdad Hotel, you could still hear your first conversation played back at you. We did not take these activities too seriously. The spoons and forks sent by the Ministry of Works to replace those looted on the day of the revolution, were sent from the office to my house. The Administrative Officer telephoned to my servant to let him know when the silver arrived. The C.I.D. appeared at my house within half an hour and, without permission, questioned the servants, believing that we were importing silver bars to give to our secret agents. Protesting about that was a pleasure. The C.I.D. car following my military attaché, nearly ran me over at the stables through careless driving. Next day the car turned up with a new driver. The occupants apologised profusely for the incident of the previous day and brought a special message that the driver was now in jail. Out shooting, the followers were useful in looking for lost birds.

We had to be careful not to compromise our many

old friends, who were naturally unwilling for a time to run the gauntlet in order to visit us, an experience well-known to all British Ambassadors in Baghdad. We had to get a pass to leave the municipal limits of Baghdad, requiring in the early days ten days' notice, though on an afternoon ride one could avoid the checkpoints. Inside Baghdad diplomatic cars were held up and on one occasion shot at by members of the Popular Resistance Force searching for weapons. We were kept busy protesting. It did not have much effect as the regular Police were not in control. It was prudent to dodge demonstrations, though they were not directed against foreigners. Throughout my stay in Baghdad, after all that had happened, there was never a demonstration against the British Embassy. With the chaos in the Government offices, in each of which there was a section favouring the Communists, it was difficult to keep the normal life of an Embassy going. We were bound up in a complicated network of passes, licences and permits, which had to be followed from office to office until the final signature was obtained. Without special pressure, a customs clearance took six months. Eight months after the revolution the Americans had been able to get liquor clearances only for milk, port and angostura bitters.

The Security Department were half on our side and we used to get tipped off when there was any particular move against us. We were continually intervening with the Military Governor-General, gradually with increasing effect. In January we had recommended that Embassy families, who had been evacuated after the revolution, should return to Baghdad, in spite of the doubts expressed in London. Provided the British had their families with them, morale remained high. In spite of the chaos and confusion, the demonstrations and the speeches, life for the foreigner was relatively peaceful. In July 1959 I was entertaining British Press correspondents in Baghdad for the celebration of the first anniversary of the revolution. I said to one correspondent that it was strange that I had just read in his newspaper a headline, 'I have just flown out of terror-stricken Baghdad'. But a few days before a British doctor, who was known to have been a close friend of the Royal Family, had remarked how quiet it had been since the revolution. I suppose we were living on the edge of a volcano, but as was remarked of the Armenians under Turkish rule at the beginning of the century, living, as people generally do in such a situation, quite comfortably.

It took a year and a half to get compensation for the death of one member of the Embassy staff, the destruction of the Embassy and the loss of property. We started by claiming £250,000, which we brought down to a little over £200,000, still something of a bargaining figure. The old house had been condemned and a new Embassy was already designed. After a year of frustrating negotiation, I sat one afternoon with Qasim for a two hours' bargaining battle. I started with £200,000, Qasim with £55,000. Each tried to make the other propose a compromise figure. Qasim blandly argued that the Embassy staff had set the Embassy on fire by burning their papers and that the whole trouble had been started by their opening fire on a peaceful crowd. Besides, he added, it was justifiable that the 'people' should burn the Embassy after the wrongs they had suffered from the British. We settled for £120,000 and the money was paid without delay. We were lucky to get it. In the atmosphere a year or two later we should have got nothing.

The Iraqis seemed to regard the burning of the Embassy as a normal political incident, of which it was not necessary to be either proud or ashamed. Many people seemed to be unaware that it was so badly damaged and for a long time thought that we were still living there. Perhaps the correct view, at least for those who had not suffered, was that of Max Mallowan, excavator of the Assyrian city of Nimrud, whom I took to see the burnt-out hulk of the building which he had known for so many years. He rubbed the wall thoughtfully with his finger. 'Not nearly so bad a fire as in some of our palaces in Nimrud,' he remarked. 'You know this has happened many times in the history of Iraq.'

4

As the Communists became stronger, they began to press home their advantage. They smashed the presses of the remaining Nationalist newspapers, which therefore disappeared for a time without Qasim having yet to break his promise not to suspend any newspaper. The Communist party newspaper now took the line that the Americans, the 'young brigands', had tried to overthrow Qasim by using Nasser to stage a revolt. But the 'old villains', the British, were the more subtle and dangerous opponents and Iraq must beware of their tricks. After the revolution 'the British Government had appointed people who had served in Iraq before and who had had contacts with so-called progressives and leftists'. I took this as a compliment and was delighted to know that they had not forgotten my efforts when I was Counsellor in Baghdad ten years before, to keep in touch with the opposition. They now overplayed their hand. They plotted a coup through Communist officers in the army and thus, for the first time, became dangerous to Qasim. He arrested some officers who had been in key positions and put non-Communist officers in their place, to weed out the party members and restore the loyalty of the affected units.

The Communists then made a determined effort to

restore the 'National Front' with their participation
and thus get representation in the Government. Many
ministers and officials signed a petition for the formation of the 'Front', being convinced that this was the
winning side. Qasim compromised by appointing four
left-wingers, one a Communist party member, to less
important Ministries. Hashim Jawad, the new Foreign
Minister, a moderate in politics, had been urging Qasim
to stop the crimes which were being committed in his
name against the Nationalist detainees. How much
Qasim had known himself was not clear. In any case, it
was now politically convenient for him to change his
position and he stopped the ill-treatment and released
many Nationalists.

It was announced that grand celebrations would be
held on the first anniversary of the revolution. It was
repugnant to us to have to celebrate the murder of the
young king, our old ally, but other countries, including
the Russians, were sending delegations and it would
have been foolish to boycott the whole affair. The Prime
Minister authorised us to attend, provided we were
satisfied that there would be nothing offensive to British
public opinion. I urged the Iraqi Foreign Minister in
this sense and kept away from one or two events, including the performance in the garden of the Palace where
the King and Crown Prince had been shot. There were
virtually no references to the past. The Communists
had the crowds out and Qasim was surrounded wherever
he went by his apparent supporters, yelling for him in
their thousands and continually interrupting his
speeches with their fulsome chanting. He evidently enjoyed it. Ever since the revolution he had been addressed
in public and in the Press as the saviour, the deliverer,
the darling of millions, phrases which probably sounded
more comic in English than in Arabic, especially when
prefaced by the title 'His Excellency' which had been
abolished at the revolution, but soon came back into

use. It was 'roses, roses all the way' and many remembered the days, only just before the revolution, when the crowds had gathered round the young king's carriage, trying to kiss his hand. From this time, Qasim appeared genuinely to believe that 'the people' loved him and to regard himself as the predestined saviour of his country.

While the celebrations were going on in Baghdad, a bloody scene was being enacted in Kirkuk, the town at the junction of the Kurdish country, in which there was also a strong Turcoman element. The processions there touched off several days of rioting and murder, almost certainly arranged by Kurdish Communists in order to terrorise their old Turcoman enemies. Qasim reacted strongly. He showed photographs of the atrocities at a Press conference and virtually accused the Communists of being responsible for the outrages. The Communist gangs were committing murders in many places. In Baghdad there were murders every few days. The extremists on both sides realised that there was now a breach between Qasim and the Communists. The Ba'athists, if we are to believe their subsequent statement, stopped plotting against Qasim, for the moment content to see the breach between him and the Communists widen. The Communist party, probably under the influence of Moscow, published a manifesto which virtually admitted their mistakes. There had, it said, been faults of leadership; some leaders had been guilty of left-wing adventurism; the party must return to orthodox courses. My Yugoslav colleague judged that the party had failed through want of discipline and organisation. They had now realised that their excesses had caused a strong reaction against them, that they had not got a sufficiently firm base among the masses to seize power and keep it and that they must revert to apparent moderation and build up their base over a long period before they could hope to get control.

The strength of the underlying Nationalist feeling in the country now reasserted itself and the Nationalists, cowed and dispirited after the Mosul revolt, began to hit back. Now Communists were murdered and in the University the Nationalists raised their heads. Baghdad and the countryside were divided into armed Communist and non-Communist sectors. The anti-Communist sectors were Ramadi district in the West on the road to Jordan, known as the black province, Mosul, most of the North outside Kurdistan, many of the southern country districts where the Communists had terrorised the population in the early days of the revolution and about half Baghdad. In the Adhamiya quarter of Baghdad no Communist could live without fear for his life. When a Nationalist youth was killed, his body was taken in procession through the streets and his photograph was posted up on the Nationalists' shops. Qasim's photograph was neutral. If Medhawi's photograph appeared by its side, the house was Communist. On a Nationalist's house it was accompanied by religious pictures or a photograph of a Nationalist killed by the Communists. There was a dangerous split through the life of the country. In the middle of August the course of events was suddenly changed. During the preceding months the officers who had openly taken part in the Mosul revolt, had been tried by Medhawi in the People's Court, but the senior officers arrested on suspicion of having been a party to it, had not been brought to trial. The Finance Minister told me later that Qasim now received information that the right-wing were preparing a coup against him with the connivance of Nasser. This could have been a Communist canard. Qasim reacted violently. At a Press conference he declared his complete confidence in Medhawi, now being heavily attacked by the Nationalists. He arrested Colonel Sirri, a senior officer in the Ministry of Defence and ordered Medhawi to try him and the two Generals,

Tabaqchali and Ukhaili, already arrested after the Mosul revolt. Medhawi sentenced Tabaqchali and Sirri to death. Tabaqchali was one of the most popular senior officers and therefore a danger to Qasim. For the first time since the constitution of the People's Court, the sentence was not unanimous, but Medhawi exercised his casting vote in favour of the death sentence.

A few batches of men directly implicated in the revolt had already been executed. One evening Baghdad Radio announced that next morning there would be executions of men who had taken part in the revolt and of some members of the old régime. No names were mentioned. General Daghestani, then under sentence of death, told me later that on that evening the prisoners from the old régime, who had been together, were separated into two batches. Neither party knew whether they would survive the night. Early next morning, there were many executions. Qasim could not be blamed for executing those who had taken part in the revolt, but he took pains to vilify them. They were shot in the presence of large numbers of Iraqi troops. The newspapers related how the wife of one of the officers had spat on her husband, as he awaited execution, out of disgust for his treason; but it was later reported that the woman had not been his wife but a prostitute brought in to act the part. Then Tabaqchali and Sirri were shot. It seems probable that Tabaqchali had known of the plot in advance, but had held his hand until he saw the outcome. Sirri was probably also privy to it, though he had not acted. But whatever the justification, it was dangerous to Qasim. They had powerful supporters who were now spurred to the point of action against him.

Lastly, four of the men of the old régime were executed, men who had harried the Communists in the past and whom they especially hated, headed by Said Qazzaz, the Kurdish Minister of the Interior under

Nuri Said. This was a sop to the Communists at a time when Qasim again needed their support. It gave them their revenge for the public execution of four of their leaders by Nuri Said in 1949. It was also an answer to Cairo Radio which had been taunting Qasim with executing Nationalists while letting off the old régime. And it might discourage Qasim's enemies. The Ministers passively accepted Qasim's decision. The one who would have fought it, Hashim Jawad, the Foreign Minister, was in New York. The Governor of Eastern Kurdistan at the time, told me later that the day before the execution, Qasim had given through him to Said Qazzaz's wife an absolute assurance that her husband would not be harmed. So Qasim forfeited the trust of those who might have been loyal to him.

Tension immediately increased and plots were hatched. At least two advanced simultaneously and separately to the last stage of planning. The Ba'athists, with help from their Syrian friends, planned to waylay Qasim's car in a narrow part of the principal street in Baghdad. Others, probably Nationalists, planned a similar operation at the house of one of Qasim's friends whom he regularly visited. That something was coming to a head in October was widely known and Iraqis were delaying the return of their families from summer holidays in the Lebanon. As usual, we heard many stories, of the Ba'athist plot from outside the country, of another from an intermediary whose request for help and money we flatly refused. We were not going to interfere in Iraq's internal affairs, for or against Qasim. The Ba'athists got in first, but failed to finish the job. The driver was killed, the A.D.C. and Qasim wounded. Qasim flattened himself on the floor of the car while his assailants who perhaps thought him dead, ran off. He had bullets in the arm and shoulder. There were more than eighty bullet holes in the car. They rushed him off to hospital. For an hour or two the situation in

the town was critical. Leading Communists collected
for safety in the Ministry of Defence. Crowds, hoping
for loot, armed with sticks, converged on Baghdad
from the mud hut encampments in which a quarter of
a million people then lived in squalor round the city.
An immediate curfew was imposed; the Army was put
on the alert; tanks and armoured cars were stationed
at strategic points. Qasim recovered sufficiently to
appear on television and show people that he was not
dead. Senior army officers who could have seized power
at this moment, remained loyal, or, more probably,
were too frightened or unorganised to act. Many Iraqis
despised them for having lost their opportunity.

Qasim settled down happily in hospital, and appeared
to enjoy receiving visits and messages of congratulation
on his escape. The car riddled with bullet holes was
placed in the courtyard of the hospital and he became
convinced that he had been specially protected by the
Almighty. He said to me: 'When they attacked me, I
smiled, for I knew that they could not kill me.' He said
that security after the attack had been wholly due to
his appearance before the microphone which had
calmed 'the people'; for 'the people love me; they kiss
the bullet-holes in the car'. Since the people loved him,
his opponents must be foreign agents of the imperialists.
He was getting into a very peculiar state of mind. When
he came out of hospital, the bloody shirt, the symbol
of divine protection, was displayed in a glass case next
to the cuckoo clock in the room in the Ministry of
Defence where Qasim received his visitors, and the car
was hoisted to a point in front of the Ministry where
it could excite the admiration of the passers-by. We
were told of plans to clear a square at the place of the
attack, in the centre of which would be erected a massive
statue of the Leader, and, at his feet, like a faithful
hound, would lie the car under an outer dome of
marble and an inner dome of glass, so arranged that the

faithful could pass round it. The glass was to be bullet-proof. The car had apparently become an extension of the Leader's personality and required protection from the imperialists.

The weeks went on. Qasim was still enjoying hospital life and all the fuss which was made of him. He was increasingly cheerful. I had fallen off a horse and had an arm in plaster. We used to compare 'our little accidents'. Curfew was relaxed and tension diminished. Iraqis began to come again to our houses. They began to ridicule their leader, but, underneath, hated and feared him. A new Ambassador arrived from the East at Basra. He was told that in Baghdad he would be living with a scorpion. People feared that once out of hospital, Qasim would turn and sting his enemies. The Ba'athists involved in the plot were known. A bullet from one side of the car had killed one of the attackers on the other side. In his pocket was a note-book with names. They cannot have been very expert conspirators. Many people, Ba'athists and others, were arrested, or fled across the frontier. Among those arrested, was a Jamaican, Marsh, employed by a British firm. Throughout the winter his fate was hanging over us. We expected that our enemies would work to attack us through the trials. At last, Qasim emerged from hospital, on a day celebrated thereafter as the 'day of safety and rejoicing', on the first anniversary with an Arabic entertainment lasting for five and a half hours without pause or refreshment. Before he left hospital, Qasim held a six-hour Press Conference at which he seemed to be again swinging towards the Communists, since he now proclaimed that the killers of Kirkuk were not Communists but Ba'athists.

During the first few months of 1960 two sets of plotters were on trial. Medhawi was brought back to try them. He was intent on trying Marsh and we had to work hard to defeat him. In the trial relating to the

Nationalists' plot one of the accused alleged that he had regularly met a British agent who used the name of 'Abu Jassim'. He also implicated in the plot the Head of the Sovereignty Council, the Chief of the General Staff and the Director of Security, all of whom we had heard had been connected with it. Qasim probably let their names come out in court to tease them and keep them under control. Our problem was to get our man out in the face of Qasim's belief that some British agency had been in a plot to murder him, which was not true. The Foreign Minister was helping us. He said to me that every Government used spies – that was understandable – but we must convince Qasim that Marsh was not a plotter. That was a very different matter. I denied that he was either.

The Minister worked on Qasim for months and at last told me that it was time to see him and advised me of the line I should take. Qasim clearly enjoyed the interview, thinking that he was in the stronger position. It took place on the day before there was any mention in court of the British agent, Abu Jassim. Neither I nor my Counsellor, Sam Falle, had ever heard of this name in connection with the case. Qasim turned to Falle who spoke Arabic, and said: 'You know Abu Jassim, don't you?' Falle replied that he knew whom Qasim meant, since it was the nickname of one of Qasim's friends, who was also on good terms with us. Qasim had been trying to trap Falle into an admission; so this needed a lot of explanation when the name came out in court the next day. However, we got what we wanted. Qasim promised that Marsh would not be prosecuted and kept his word. Marsh was brought as a witness, although he was ill and unable to stand, and was repeatedly attacked by Medhawi as a British spy, but Medhawi was not allowed to try him. We pressed for his release, helped by an intervention from the Prime Minister of Jamaica. At last, he was allowed to go home. The firm which had employed him, tidied up his belongings which had been gone through by the Iraqi Police. In the bottom of a box was a tommy gun and ammunition. The Iraqi Police were not very thorough.

The Ba'athists were sentenced to death. No one could contest the justice of the sentence. At the end of Ramadan, the month of fasting during which by custom no one is executed, Qasim decided to hang them. The evening before the day fixed for the execution, he still maintained his decision. A meeting of the Council of Ministers started at 10 p.m. The story was spread around that the Ba'athists threatened immediate revenge if their men should die. What made Qasim change his mind, I do not know. At midnight he started to deliver a two-hour speech on the Radio. Much of it was economic detail, including the reason for the increase in the price of meat. Suddenly, at the end, he said that he had been intending to hang the prisoners in a few hours, but since it was a Friday and the end of the holy month, he had decided to reprieve them. He had never announced that he was going to execute them. Why he found it necessary to say that he had changed his mind, no one understood. The decision to reprieve them was probably political. The new 'Martial Courts' had sentenced to death a number of Communists for the murder of non-Communists. The Soviet Press and Radio, under pressure from Arab Communists, were pressing for their reprieve. Qasim did not want to execute the Ba'athists and reprieve the Communists. He did not want to execute the Communists for fear of a final breach with them. So he did nothing and left both under sentence of death. It was the familiar policy of balance. The Ba'athists were never executed. In the end, they got him.

5

O_N 6 January 1960, Qasim proclaimed the end of the 'transitional period' and the immediate licensing of political parties. It was soon apparent that it was only a trick to create a political façade behind which he would continue to keep all the power to himself. The Ba'athists were underground. The Independence Party, the Nationalist opposition before the revolution, refused to apply. The old left-wing opposition, the National Democrats, were licensed, but soon disintegrated. Two Nationalist splinter parties were refused licences. One appealed successfully to the Supreme Court, but was suppressed in a few months and went underground. The Communists applied. Qasim licensed a tame Communist in his pay. The official Communist party was only a bad joke. The real Communists went underground. The Kurdish party was licensed. Its leaders were in Qasim's pay. They ceased to trust him and went off to Kurdistan. Soon, all that was left of the grand political design were the Finance Minister and one or two of his business friends under a fancy name and Qasim's tame Communist who represented only himself and Qasim.

No one would have minded much if the administration had worked properly, but it went rapidly downhill from its high standard before the revolution. Qasim decided everything himself. He exhausted his Ministers by starting meetings late in the evening and continuing all night, filling the time with long monologues. The Ministers were generally despised. A friend of one of them told him that he could understand their staying up all night for gambling or women, but to spend every night sitting at a table opposite that madman was incomprehensible. The Development Board was replaced by a Department staffed by Communists and fellow-travellers. Their plans were no more than a jumble of projects without priorities or relation to available resources. Projects were selected by Qasim on prestige grounds. The reports of the new East European advisers joined the old reports in the pigeon-holes. Land reform collapsed. Irrigation projects started by the old régime were proclaimed as triumphs of the new. The cost of development and administration soared.

It was difficult for the Russians too. The Soviet Ambassador said to me that Nuri had made many mistakes, but at least you could rely on what he said. You never knew where you were with Qasim. The administration, he said, was hopelessly inefficient and when he went to Qasim to discuss practical problems, he was treated to endless discourses on the triumphs of the revolution. At first the Russian experts were not so good and, with all the fringe benefits and interpreters required, cost as much as the Westerners. Their medical efforts were a failure. It was not much good sending a party to do mass vaccinations, when the most lowly Iraqi medical assistants had been doing them for years. Their doctors were not up to the Iraqi doctors with their F.R.C.S. degrees from London or Edinburgh. Perhaps, we thought, they believed their own propaganda about the conditions created by imperialism. The Russian doctors quickly disappeared. So did the pilots and engineers brought in to replace the British in the Basra port. The irrigation engineers were only working over old ground. It had all been planned before. What was required was to put some of the plans into effect. Estimates for Russian factories came under criticism and there were complaints about the agricultural machinery and military equipment. Visits to Moscow, forbidden before the revolution, were disenchanting. Iraqis still preferred to pay the London Clinic rather than get free treatment in Moscow.

The Russians, having been the popular heroes of the early days of the revolution, lost their favoured position. The excesses and failure of the local Communists did not help them. But they still made progress. They brought in better experts and reduced prices. They got the contract for widening the gauge of the Baghdad-Basra railway. They did it all on cheap credit, and who knew what would have happened before the time came to repay the loans? There was a continual flow to the Soviet Union of officers for training in the new weapons and of students to the Universities, not all of whom came back unconvinced. Russian arms flowed in and the old military mission was still there – only it was now Russian. The Russians' chief asset was Qasim. He remained convinced that the West was his real enemy and he needed Russian help. There were still Communists among his closest companions. He pressed Russian tenders on his reluctant officials. Moscow gave him full political support, whatever he did to the local Communists, and never attacked him personally. They knew that the local Communists would not be able to take power soon. They could only work for the future. Meanwhile, they could work effectively on Qasim. After three years, they were well dug in with hundreds of technicians in the country, reinforced by competent English-speaking Czechs and Poles, and became a prominent feature of the Iraqi landscape.

An Egyptian cartoon showed Qasim at the head of

his troops shouting 'left-right, left-right', with the caption, 'Make up your mind'. His policy was, simply, to play off one side against the other, acting against any-one who threatened him. He had no political convic-tions except to stay in power. He trusted no one and no one trusted him. When each party realised that they could not capture him and that he was the only winner in this game, they became progressively less inclined to play. So in the end he isolated himself and retained the support only of those who would fall with him. For the moment, he had defeated the Ba'athist and Nationalist attempts to kill him, and both parties were split. The Shia leaders, the political priests in the South, were openly against him, but they no longer had the power which they had in the twenties, when they could rouse the tribes and bring down a Government. The army's tanks had changed that.

Now it was the Communists' turn to suffer. The Provincial Governors and Police gradually recovered their authority. The Communist newspapers were suppressed and many Communists arrested and put into detention camps. The Popular Resistance Force was abolished and to balance the pro-Communist People's Court, political anti-Communist 'martial courts' began to convict the Communists responsible for the murders at Mosul and Kirkuk in the days of their power. The Government changed sides in the elections to the governing committees of the Trade Unions and profes-sional associations, which now became anti-Communist. In Mosul the anti-Communists took their revenge. Communists and their friends were shot in the streets, first after dark and later in the daytime. The Police did not intervene. The avengers were said to have stuck the heads of three Communist supporters on the bonnet of their car and rolled the car down into their village. In Baghdad they placed a body with its severed head carefully balanced on top, on a chair on the spot where

Qasim took the salute on 14 July. The Police now fired without fear of retribution on rioters in the streets. New prison camps were built and there were probably more in detention than under the old régime. But Qasim never came out openly against the Communists and he was still the best Prime Minister whom they could hope for.

Qasim now concentrated on making it difficult for anyone to kill him. He used a bullet-proof car presented by the Russians and later, since it was unsatisfactory, a bullet-proof Cadillac. He was always escorted by one or more truck-loads of soldiers. His new apartment in the Ministry of Defence had bullet-proof windows. At official parties he was surrounded by military police carrying arms, who arrived before the guests and bounced up and down on the sofas and chairs to test them for bombs. At official ceremonies no one was allowed anywhere near him. He had at least six intelligence services, spying on each other and every-one else. He transferred any senior officer who was getting too popular in his district. He allowed no unit to fall into the control of either Communists or Nationalists. The Air Force Commander was a Com-munist; directly under him were two staunch Nation-alists. The Commander of the second division in the North was a Nationalist; his brigade commander in Nationalist Mosul was a Communist, and so everywhere Communist and anti-communist officers were en-couraged to spy on each other. The Security officials spied on the top generals. Power was in the hands of Qasim's personal agents.

So it was on the civil side also. Some Ministers were for, some against the Communists. Some Ministries were captured by the Communists, some by the Nationalists. The Communist leaders were under-ground. The police probably knew where they were, but did not arrest them. Any newspaper could now attack its opponents, provided it supported Qasim and was anti-imperialist. Qasim paid newspapers to attack his friends or his enemies, according to his tactical needs of the moment. A press attack against a Minister was the signal that he must toe the line if he wanted to keep his job or that he was on the way out. All the senior officers with personality were retired, and the younger officers were kept more or less loyal with houses, television sets and cars on easy terms. Qasim was not a doctrinaire socialist. The businessman could make a fortune, provided he supported Qasim, who allowed his relations and supporters to do very well.

Every month we would hear of a new plot, often with the names of the plotters and the date proposed. On the third anniversary of the revolution Qasim announced that he had scotched twenty-seven plots against him. On the Shah's birthday in the spring of 1961, it was expected that Qasim would, as usual, attend the Iranian Ambassador's party. The military police were waiting for him. A young Ba'athist came up to a member of my staff and said: 'Look out; they are going for him here, don't get too close.' Qasim did not come. Presumably, he had heard too. We could not stop people coming to us and telling us about their plots. One said that the tribes were ready and part of the Air Force squared. All they wanted was money and a promise of support for the new Government. Another said: 'It's all fixed; all we want is £50,000 for the family, in case it goes wrong.' They were all told that there was nothing doing, and that we could have nothing to do with them. Some may have been sent by Qasim to try and trip us up; but in any case we were not going to get involved in any plot.

Most people were against the plots. For life was better now than at any time since the revolution. A new coup would only mean more chaos. Even in Mosul, where the killing of Communists had developed into murder on private account, things were quietening down. The break-up of the Egyptian-Syrian union had removed the danger of Egyptian-sponsored revolt. In 1961 the remaining prisoners of the old régime, the Ba'athists who had tried to kill Qasim, Abdul Salam Arif and Rashid Ali Gailani and most of the other detainees were released and came out in fairly good shape. Things were looking up. And what was the use of revolution if all it meant was substituting one stupid soldier for another? But the danger of a coup remained until the Ba'athists finally killed Qasim. His Foreign Minister told me he had said to him: 'If you have a Cabinet, a Parliament and a proper delegation of powers, no one will want to kill you.' His Finance Minister, almost his only supporter now among the politicians, said to me that in Iraq a political party could only work underground. We were back to the days of Nuri Said, with the difference that Nuri had had some support among the landlords and reactionaries. And, I added, Nuri had sat on the lid too long and was blown up.

Qasim continually promised a return to political life, but no one believed him. He remained the 'sole leader', as he liked to be called, taking no advice, relying on his own cunning and keeping everything in his hands. There had long since ceased to be any popular manifestations in his favour. The Communists were no longer prepared to organise the street for him, and his car passed without notice. His photographs in the streets were put up by the Police. But he remained as much of a narcissist as ever. His room was filled with portraits and busts of himself. He did not appear to mind who put up pictures of him, provided there were plenty of them. He would listen with a rapt look on his face to re-broadcasts of his speeches. He published an account of how he had taken the oil company's representatives on a tour in the poorer quarters of Baghdad, while he went without guards among the people, who received him with joy and devotion. He kept visitors waiting for hours and ignored official appointments while he developed his latest theme to anyone who happened to be seeing him. In the streets they called him the bulbul because he made so many speeches. No one listened to them any more except to try and find out what the man would be up to next. Yet this unattractive man, so lacking in charm, so uninspired, so wrapped up in his own conceit, so insufferably self-righteous, with God firmly on his side, a bit crazy with his mad, staring eyes, succeeded in holding his position and in keeping himself alive for four and a half years by cunning and a single-minded devotion to the maintenance of his power. In the end, this was all that the Iraqi revolution was about.

6

An oil company is in perpetual negotiation with the host Government. Up to the revolution, the negotiations between the Iraq Petroleum Company and the Iraqi Government had not always been easy, but they had been conducted on the basis of recognition of the validity of the concession and with good-will on both sides. There had been some arguments. The Iraqi Government had complained that the Company had been slow to train Iraqis to hold responsible positions, to modify the concession to accord with changing times, to explore and develop the country's large oil resources sufficiently vigorously and to recognise the importance of its relationship with the Iraqi Government. These complaints ignored many of the difficulties facing the Company, which had however done its best to meet them. The Company's business had been conducted in London and its local headquarters had been placed not in Baghdad but in the more salubrious climate of Tripoli at the Mediterranean end of the pipeline. But, in due course, sensible administrative changes were made. Important functions were transferred from London and the local office was moved to Baghdad. Iraqi oil royalties rose to £90 million a year. Work was started which would double oil production in three years, including the building of a deep-sea terminal some miles out to sea in the Gulf.

What I refer to as the Iraq Petroleum Company, was a group consisting of the 'Iraq, Mosul and Basra Petroleum Companies', which operated virtually as one company. By 1938, as a result of successive negotiations it had acquired concessions covering practically the whole country. However new negotiations had been started with a view to the relinquishment of some areas. Negotiations were not made easier by the structure of the company which was owned by Shell, British Petroleum, Standard Oil of New Jersey, Socony Mobil, the Compagnie Francaise de Pétrole and the Gulben-kian interests. After the revolution the Company was officially attacked as an imperialist monopoly which, under the protection of the British Government and a reactionary régime, had sucked the wealth of the country and exploited Iraq's resources in its own selfish interests. The Ministry of Oil was successively in the hands of two fellow-travellers, the first of whom, in a period of eighteen months in office, visited no oilfield except Baku. The Company managed to carry on nor-mal production in conditions of great difficulty caused by the communist-dominated Trade Union and arrests of its employees after the Mosul revolt; but expansion was seriously delayed by local conditions and uncer-tainty about the future.

Negotiations for a revision of the concession continued intermittently with Qasim and his ministers for three years, being concentrated for the first two years on relinquishment of concession areas. The argu-ment began on percentages. 25% crept up to 50%. Qasim lifted it to 59%. The Company agreed. Qasim lifted it again. He calculated correctly that he could push them further. He had pushed as far as this with-out conceding the Company's condition that they should choose the areas to be given up, which made all the difference. Qasim dragged out the negotiations and spread rumours that he was going to nationalise the Company. He had no intention of doing so. Two thirds of his revenues came from oil. If the oil stopped, he would fall. In the summer of 1960, at the Company's request, I intervened to break a deadlock. Both sides now agreed to a new formula by which the Company would give up 75% at once and be left with 10% after fourteen years. Qasim was enjoying his own cleverness. He reopened the whole discussion, kept the Managing Director waiting for weeks and broke off the negotiations.

At this point he began to widen the scope of the discussions, saying that all points were links in a chain and must be settled together. Months were spent on the question whether dead-rents paid to the Iraqi Government before oil was found, should be treated as a taxable expense. Then rights to flared-off gas were brought in and argument developed over the unilateral raising of the agreed Basra Port dues on exported oil. Finally, a list of twelve demands by the Iraqis emerged, including share participation and an increase of the 50/50 Government's share of profits. The arguments were long and complicated. Qasim was still pushing the Company up and refusing to settle. In August 1961, when the political atmosphere had deteriorated, a high-level delegation from the Groups took up the discussions. The Iraqi minister now proposed an immediate relinquishment of 90% and a joint venture in the portion of the remaining 10% which had not been exploited. The Company might even have agreed to this, but Qasim coupled with it a change in the 50/50 ratio. The negotiations finally broke down. A law was passed expropriating the whole area of the concession outside the wells actually producing oil. This removed from the Company about half the valuable Rumeila field which they had discovered.

It might have been possible to get an agreement on generous terms soon after the revolution when Qasim was not sure of himself, though it is doubtful whether the Company could, at any time, have taken the matter through the long process of negotiations, initialling, signature and ratification of the agreement. Later there was never a chance. Qasim was clever up to a point, but then overplayed his hand. He did no service to his country. As a result of his tactics production stagnated and Iraq lost many millions of pounds in royalties which they could have obtained if Qasim had been prepared to deal reasonably with the Company.

7

On 25 June 1961, Qasim laid claim to Kuwait. The Ottoman Empire had claimed suzerainty over it, but there had never been a Turkish administration there. When in 1899 Mubarak as Sabah of Kuwait murdered his brothers, he sought protection with the Turkish Government which gave him the honorary title of Qaimaqam or sub-Governor of a district, and included Kuwait in their reports, but not in fact, in the district of Basra. He subsequently appealed to the British Government who gave him their protection in return for his accepting limitations on his sovereignty. The British power was the stronger; the Turkish Government were unable to extend their authority beyond Basra, and Kuwait continued to be regarded, as it always had been, as a part of the Gulf territories and not as part of Iraq. In 1913 the British Government and the Porte signed an agreement which recognised Turkish sovereignty over Kuwait, on the express condition that Turkish administration was not extended to it; but the agreement was not ratified owing to the outbreak of war. In 1914, after the war began, the Resident in the Gulf encouraged the Sheikh to attack the Turks in the Basra area, and in November 1914, when the British occupied Basra, the Sheikh's independence was formally recognised under British protection and subject to the 1899 agreement.

In 1920, on the establishment of the mandate over Iraq, the Iraqi boundaries excluded Kuwait. In 1922 Sir Percy Cox negotiated with Saudi Arabia the boundary between Kuwait and Saudi Arabia, Kuwait giving up its claim to areas to the South and West of Kuwait proper, and one area being declared as a neutral zone, under the sovereignty of Saudi Arabia and Kuwait. In 1932 Nuri Said, then Prime Minister of Iraq, in agreeing to the conditions for Iraq's independence, confirmed the boundaries of the mandated territory as the boundaries of independent Iraq. In 1938 King Ghazi orally laid claim to Kuwait, but the claim was rejected. The boundary between Iraq and Kuwait was never fully demarcated. In the spring of 1958 the Iraqi Government ran into difficulties over the union with Jordan and needed the adhesion of Kuwait in order to meet criticisms that the only result of the union was to divert Iraqi revenues to meet the Jordanian deficit. The Sheikh was reluctant to join; so Nuri Said tried to put pressure on him by claiming not the whole of Kuwait on a historical basis, but the islands in the north of Kuwait territory, on the ground that they were in Iraqi territorial waters. This claim was overtaken by the revolution.

During the first three years of the revolution, the Iraqi Government made no claim and their actions suggested that they recognised Kuwait as a separate State. In December 1958 they asked Kuwait to agree to their having a consul there. On a number of occasions they addressed letters to the Government of Kuwait, in terms implying that it was not part of Iraq. Only a month before Qasim's claim, a Kuwaiti delegation had signed a trade agreement with Iraq and a communiqué was issued referring to the two brotherly countries. Kuwait, with Iraqi support, had become a member of a number of international specialised agencies, and only two weeks before the claim, the Iraqi representative spoke in favour of Kuwait's membership of the International Labour Organisation, saying that he welcomed to the international field the adherence of a younger Arab brother who was already part of the Arab family. On Iraqi initiative the 'Organisation of Petroleum Exporting Countries' was established with Kuwait as one of the founder members. Kuwait was also a member of several technical committees of the Arab League, and at a meeting held only a few months before in Baghdad, had been accepted as a member of the proposed Arab Bank and Arab Air Line. If Kuwait had not yet achieved full international status, it was because it was still under British protection under the 1899 Agreement. Its status as a separate territory was fully recognised.

In the course of 1960 the Sheikh of Kuwait represented to the British Government that the agreement of 1899 was out of date and asked to have it revised. Negotiations continued until the middle of 1961 and were referred to in the Kuwaiti Press, but the Iraqis raised no objection. In April 1961 Qasim in a public speech referred with scorn to a wholly unfounded story that Kuwait would join the British Commonwealth, ridiculing the idea on the ground that there was no connection between Kuwait and Britain. He referred to the old links between Iraq and Kuwait before and after the 1914–18 war and to there being no boundaries between Iraq and Kuwait. I asked the Foreign Minister the meaning of these references. He replied that they were purely historical. I heard afterwards that my German colleague had asked the Foreign Minister the same question and had been treated to a lecture on the wickedness of the British in separating Kuwait from Iraq; but that when the Ambassador had asked the Foreign Minister what would be done about the Iraqi claim that Iraq and Kuwait were one country, he had been told that it was up to the Sheikh of Kuwait.

We did not consider Qasim's reference to be of significance. The Iraqi Government had been stressing the concept of the Arab family, and the reference to the boundaries was thought to be only a term of Arab politeness between neighbours. The Government of Saudi Arabia had used the same phrase in reference to Kuwait. About this time, I told the Iraqi Foreign Minister, on behalf of the Kuwaiti Government, that Kuwait was agreeable in principle to accept consuls from the United Arab Republic and Iraq. Arrangements were in hand to train Kuwaitis in Iraq for the Kuwaiti Foreign Service. The Foreign Minister also told me that they would reply in a few weeks to a letter from the Kuwaiti Government asking for the establishment of a joint body to demarcate the Iraq-Kuwait boundary and implied that they would agree. I replied to his enquiry that I knew nothing about the reported negotiations being held in London with a view to Kuwaiti independence and said that we already regarded Kuwait as independent. I asked him how Iraq would view Kuwait's independence. He replied that they would welcome the emergence to independence of any Arab State. When I reminded him of this later, he neither denied it nor tried to suggest that he had not been referring to Kuwait. The Minister of Finance told me later that the Foreign Minister had no right to say this, having heard Qasim express his views on Kuwait a number of times in the Council of Ministers.

At the beginning of June 1961 I was told of the projected Anglo-Kuwaiti agreement. The text was ready for signature. Before signing it, the Sheikh wanted to know how we thought Qasim would react. I was asked my opinion. I replied that it was by no means certain that Qasim would react adversely, since he had recently been addressing the Sheikh in a very friendly manner.

But it depended on his mood at the moment how he would receive the news. I recommended that the agreement should not be announced until the Iraqi Foreign Minister returned from an Arab League meeting in Cairo and that I should be allowed to tell him beforehand. This, I thought, might diminish the chances of a hostile reaction. Fortunately, my recommendation was not accepted. The Political Agent objected that signature of the agreement could not be postponed any longer, since it was already becoming public knowledge and signature and publication had been fixed for 19 June.

I was authorised to tell the Iraqi Government on that evening. Qasim was acting as Foreign Minister. I did not go and see him, since I did not want to suggest that the agreement was of any great importance. We regarded it as merely regularising the existing position. Moreover, there was a crisis in the affairs of the Iraq Petroleum Company at that moment. I could not speak for the Company and did not want to get involved. I therefore gave the text of the agreement to the senior official in the Foreign Ministry. He made no comment nor reserved the Iraqi Government's position. He told me a few days later that he had taken my communication to Qasim with a draft telegram to the Sheikh congratulating him on his independence. Qasim had torn up the draft and had dictated a telegram to the Sheikh congratulating him on having got rid of the false agreement of 1899, but saying nothing about his independence.

Others also misjudged Qasim's reaction. The Iraqi Minister of Commerce was representing Iraq at a meeting of the Arab Economic Council at Damascus, at which Kuwait was separately represented. He joined the other Arab Ministers in sending a telegram of congratulations to the Sheikh. The Arab League meeting in Cairo had ended and the Foreign Minister

was in Beirut on his way home. He did not appear to
have thought this a critical moment, since he did not
return to Baghdad until three days later. In my first
interview with him after Qasim had made his claim,
he complained that the agreement had been announced
while he was away, adding that hazard plays a great
part in international affairs; but he was in Baghdad for
three days before the Press Conference and the senior
official in the Foreign Ministry was probably right when
he said to me that it would have made no difference if
the Minister had been in Baghdad at the time of the
announcement of the agreement. We heard later that
he had asked Qasim whether his Press Conference
would be about Kuwait and was only told: 'You'll
see.' In these days the other Arab Governments began
to announce their recognition of Kuwait's independence.

On the evening of Sunday 25 June, we were at an
official cocktail party when the news came that Qasim
had laid claim to Kuwait, declaring that on the next
day by Republican Decree the Sheikh would be
appointed Qaimaqam of Kuwait which was a part of the
Basra district. It was more than a claim. It was a declaration that Kuwait no longer existed, but was a part of
Iraq. There was nothing about pursuing the claim by
peaceful means. On the contrary, the assumption was
that, since Kuwait was a part of Iraq, Iraqi troops could
move in as a normal measure of internal security within
their jurisdiction. Probably only a few senior officers
concerned with the planning knew what Qasim was
going to do. At the time of the Press Conference there
was a party at the house of the Chief of the General
Staff at which all the Ministers in Baghdad were
present. The Director General of the Army Medical
Services who was there, told me that they were all
surprised.

There can be no doubt that Qasim had every intention of following up his claim. He instructed the Minister of Housing to visit Kuwait and draw up plans for housing projects there. A senior official in the Ministry of Finance had his leave stopped on the ground that he would be required to draw up a revised budget incorporating Kuwait. It was announced that Kuwaitis in Iraq would no longer be required to conform to the regulations for foreigners in Iraq and a foreigner wanting to visit Kuwait was told that he would not need an exit permit from Iraq. And soon there was evidence of troop movements.

The situation developed dangerously. Qasim's pet newspaper was alleging that Iraqis were being persecuted by imperialist agents in Kuwait and it looked as if a campaign was being mounted to justify intervention. At the same time, we began to get reliable information that the first tank regiment was moving to Basra. We were soon hearing stories that a large number of troops had been moved South under cover of the two all-night rehearsals of the 14 July parade. We knew that a senior officer in the tank regiment had gone to Basra to arrange accommodation for the regiment. While he was away, a relation confirmed that he was in Basra. On his return, we managed to get into touch with him under the pretext that we wanted to rent his house, and he admitted, when cornered, in a high state of nerves, that the regiment was preparing to move and that railway 'flats' were being collected. My Military Attaché, with a touch of genius, went up to a senior railway official at a party and said to him: 'Why did you allow your rolling stock to be used for moving the tanks?' Caution having been suspended by several whiskies, the official replied: 'Yes, I am very angry. They arranged it through my subordinates without telling me.'

We had plenty of evidence. Iraqis told us of hearing from friends that members of their families in the regiment in question were in Basra. The attachés on the morning 'milk run', as we used to call it, confirmed that the tanks had gone. Later, the Iraqi military attaché from London attacked my attachés for spreading false rumours of troop movements, but admitted that the tanks had moved, though not to Basra. By this time, as we knew, they had been moved back into the interior. We knew too that a Task Force had been constituted and the name of its Commander and that forward parties of units of several divisions had been moved down. There were large orders for petrol, including aviation spirit. Kurdish soldiers who were not part of the garrison, were seen in the Basra bazaar before being moved out. The road from Basra towards Kuwait was widened at night for heavy traffic. Railway wagons were requisitioned. There was plenty of evidence that the Task Force was to be a reinforced Brigade with guns, tanks and air support.

The Press and Radio were giving totally untrue accounts of the situation in Kuwait, apparently based on Qasim's false expectations. A day or two after the Press Conference, a British Press correspondent came by air from Kuwait to Basra. He told me that the aircraft was met by a man from Baghdad Radio who asked an Iraqi passenger whether there had been demonstrations in Kuwait on the previous day. 'Yes,' said the passenger. 'Were they shouting for Abdul Karim Qasim?' 'No; for the Sheikh.' 'Were they carrying photographs?' 'Yes.' 'Of Abdul Karim Qasim?' 'No; of the Sheikh.' The interviewer gave up, but that did not prevent Baghdad Radio reporting vast demonstrations in Kuwait in favour of Qasim. It looked as if Qasim intended to use force. I went to the Foreign Ministry, my Military Attaché to the Ministry of Defence. We made it plain to the Iraqis that, if necessary, we would carry out our obligations to the Sheikh of Kuwait and that they must reckon on this. I telegraphed to London that we must make sure that

Qasim would not get to Kuwait before we were ready and I asked that the Commando carrier, Bulwark, which was due to arrive off Kuwait on 4 July, should go there immediately. I asked to be given ample warning if it was decided that British troops were to go into Kuwait, since it might mean a breach of diplomatic relations, and that the Swiss should be alerted to take charge of our interests if this happened.

The morale of the Iraqi troops was low and their training and maintenance was indifferent. In Baghdad we thought that an Iraqi attack, even if carried out at night, could be dealt with by air reconnaissance and an air attack from Bahrain, followed by reinforcements of ground troops. If we put ground troops into Kuwait while Qasim was still getting his Task Force ready, he would be able to attack us as imperialists occupying an Arab State without any threat from Iraq, and might make political capital against us in the Arab world. We therefore suggested that we defer putting British ground troops into Kuwait until Qasim started to make an overt move. The British Government, however, having the War Office's assessment of Iraqi military preparations and having Kuwaiti morale in mind, decided to send in British ground troops in advance. Since an Iraqi move over the border would mean only a fifty mile drive to Kuwait town, which could probably be made at night, and in view of the difficulties which our Forces would face if Qasim got there first, they considered that it was not safe to rely on air strikes.

On 1 July British troops moved in. We started burning our papers. But there was no breach of relations. The official Iraqi reaction was to send a Note to all diplomatic Missions in Baghdad attacking the British action, reasserting the Iraqi claim and denying the validity of the Anglo-Kuwaiti agreement. Now for the first time the Iraqi Government specifically denied that they had any intention of using force and declared categorically that not a man nor a tank had been moved. The Foreign Minister told me that there had been a plan to move a tank regiment to the South as part of a reorganisation scheme worked out some months before. Knowing that this would cause misunderstandings, he had intervened and stopped it. It is possible that Qasim had told him that nothing had been moved and that he believed it. When Qasim suggested to the Indian Ambassador that he should send his Military Attaché to Basra to see for himself, we knew that Qasim had dropped the preparation of the Task Force, at least for the time being, that the tanks were now well hidden and that there was nothing more to see.

In the light of the evidence that we now collected, we made our assessment. It seemed most probable that Qasim had been intending to acquire Kuwait by a coup timed for completion on 14 July, the third anniversary of the revolution. He seems to have been told that he had only to announce his claim to Kuwait for a majority of the population to declare in his favour. He planned to create his special Task Force under cover of the rehearsals for the 14 July parade. The alleged plan of reorganisation may have been designed as a cover for troop movements. As soon as the Force was in position at about the end of June, he would have made his declaration and, on some excuse, would have sent his Task Force to complete the job. He probably calculated that once he was in Kuwait, he could hold the position and that the British, with the experience of Suez, would not try and eject him.

The agreement of 19 June took him by surprise. Within a few days after the announcement, he realised that the political basis for his action was being undermined by the recognition of Kuwait by other Arab States. He had therefore to make his declaration or see the position further eroded. His Task Force was not ready, but he probably thought that if he blew his trumpets, the walls of Jericho would fall of their own accord. Perhaps he did not regard the British undertaking to Kuwait as serious. He sent observers to Kuwait to watch reactions, went ahead with his Task Force and started a Press campaign about atrocities in Kuwait to give his Forces an excuse to move in 'to protect Iraqi nationals'. The population of Kuwait demonstrated in favour of the Sheikh; the Arab States maintained their support of Kuwait's independence; the British showed that they were serious. For the moment, therefore, the game was up. He called off the operation and covered up his tracks. We had failed to spot what he was up to; but then so had everyone else who was not involved in the plot. We had had a bit of luck. If the Anglo-Kuwaiti agreement had been delayed, the plan might have got further on Qasim's time-table, though I doubt whether it could ever have been successful. But it would have been much more trouble to scotch. The agreement dislocated his plans.

British in Iraq; so we asked for it to be damped down again, to get the right impression of strength without aggressiveness. Qasim maintained his claim and reiterated that he had never intended to use force. He tried to weaken Arab support for Kuwait, but was defeated by the decision to admit Kuwait to the Arab League and to send an Arab Force to replace the British.

Throughout the celebrations of the third anniversary of the revolution, Qasim was engaged in violent attacks on the British. He attacked the other Arab States for being misled by the British. To any delegation visiting him he would discourse for hours on his claim. One evening he kept two thousand people waiting for two hours while he explained it all to some visiting Pakistanis. I kept away from most of the ceremonies, but went to the opening of an extension to the Baghdad refinery, which had been put up by a British firm, a fact which was not once mentioned during the proceedings. Qasim started on his usual tirade against the British. I did not want to give him the satisfaction of making me walk out; it was better not to take him seriously. But I went up to him afterwards and said: 'Prime Minister, you are getting very angry with us. Don't you think we should talk about it?' The next day I was asked to go and see him. He was quite amiable, expounding his claim at length and producing his documents and maps like a child exhibiting his new toys. I said that he presumably knew what people in Baghdad were saying. It was going around that he and I had cooked up the Kuwait affair together; to which he replied that the Iraqis were very clever at finding out what lay beneath the surface. I said that we did not threaten Iraq, but had acted only in accordance with our obligation to the Ruler of Kuwait. Qasim threatened that if we did not alter our position, British interests would suffer. It went on for two hours. The

Yugoslav Ambassador was kept waiting for three hours to pay his farewell visit and nearly went home.

At this time Qasim was talking about the Iraqi boundaries as being 'From the North of Zakko (on the Turkish frontier) to the South of Kuwait'. From what he and the Foreign Minister were saying to visitors, it now looked as if the Iraqis were claiming not only Kuwait, but also the area given to the Saudis by Sir Percy Cox's decision of 1922, some Saudi territory to the south of this and even perhaps some of the Aramco fields in the Saudi coastal provinces. It looked as if they might have vague ambitions to pick up the Gulf when the British left it. The Foreign Minister had been opposed to Qasim's method of pursuing his claim to Kuwait, if not to his claim itself. He had contemplated resignation after Qasim's Press conference. He and his Ministry did not believe in the legal validity of the claim. He said to an Iraqi friend that Qasim had a hundred documents to prove his claim, but they were none of them any good, and a senior official of the Ministry confessed to me that the claim was full of holes. We had indications that the Minister's own plan had been to revive Nuri Said's claim to the northern part of Kuwait territory, on geographical rather than historical grounds. He made it clear that he would resign if force were used. He argued to me that we should have expected Qasim's reaction to the agreement, ignoring his own previous statement. I replied that the whole mess was the result of Iraq's not conducting an open policy, but preferring secrecy and conspiracy.

Qasim had spoilt the Foreign Minister's efforts to improve Iraq's relations with the other Arab States and promote general inter-Arab co-operation. The Minister had taken the initiative towards the resumption of relations with Jordan. He had succeeded in bringing to Baghdad for a meeting of the Arab League's political committee Dr Fawzi, the Foreign Minister of the United Arab Republic, paying the first official visit by an Egyptian to Iraq for many years, and the Foreign Minister of Tunis, which had refused to go to Arab League meetings since Borguiba had accused Nasser of trying to murder him. He had made some real progress in promoting Arab economic co-operation on a basis of equality. He had earned an officially inspired Egyptian attack to the effect that under imperialist influence the vigour and force of Arab policy (i.e. Nasser's policy) was 'being diluted by Jordanian Hashemitism and Qasimite opportunism'. Now this policy was in ruins. The Arab States had opposed Iraq over Kuwait; the British were about to withdraw behind an Arab shield, and Iraq could do no more than absent herself from Arab League meetings. The Minister's dream of building an Arab Commonwealth had ceased to be practical politics. The Kuwait issue had brought to the fore all the conflicts of interest of the Arab States and Arab disunity was once more convincingly demonstrated.

Qasim's attitude now changed to bitter resentment, arising from the frustration of his plans. In August, on my return from a few days in London, I gave Qasim a message, sent on my suggestion, repeating our desire for friendly relations with Iraq and again denying that there was any threat from the British Forces in Kuwait. It was a bad day for Qasim. On that morning the news had been published that the Arab Force for Kuwait, about which many doubts had been expressed, would definitely be formed. This destroyed Qasim's last hope, that the British retreat would not be covered by the Arab League and that we would find it increasingly difficult to go or to stay. He replied that the British had stabbed Iraq in the back and that every action taken by the British Government since the revolution had been hostile to Iraq. There was now no dealing with him. I continued my talks with the Foreign Minister. He wanted British-Iraqi talks on Kuwait. I replied that negotiations could only be between Iraq and independent Kuwait and that they could not take place so long as Qasim maintained his claim. The Jordanians, whose attitude had been equivocal, since they looked to Iraq to support them against Nasser and always had the 'fertile crescent' in mind, now proposed a federation of Jordan, Iraq and Kuwait. The Iraqis refused to consider it. So the Jordanians switched to support of Kuwait, especially since Nasser showed signs of wanting to bail out, and perhaps in the hope of getting a loan from Kuwait in payment for their support. The political deadlock remained.

The Iraqi public did not appear to care. There were no demonstrations of support for Qasim. Qasim's move was a fiasco and with its failure he lost prestige at home. If he had succeeded, every Iraqi would have acclaimed him. Now they were confirmed in their impression that he was a fool. We had to show that we had an effective deterrent, but at the same time to present the dispute as an inter-Arab affair. As usual, putting troops into a country was not too difficult. The problem was to get them out again. In London people had been suggesting that the Arab Force was not going to be strong enough to deter the Iraqis. In Baghdad we believed that the political deterrent was strong enough and that it would be fatal for us to reject the Arab Force and stay ourselves. The Ruler of Kuwait settled this by making it clear that he wanted the Arab not the British deterrent to stay. Then it was suggested that we should make open arrangements for the return of our Forces to Kuwait in case of need and emphasise publicly our undertaking to come to the aid of the Ruler if asked to do so, referring to this undertaking in replying to a question about the need for buildings for our Forces in Bahrain. But the Iraqis knew well enough what Forces we had in Bahrain and it was not wise to advertise that the

Arab Force had a contingent British backing. That might have raised a demand for abrogation of the new Anglo-Kuwaiti Agreement as a condition for the establishment of an Arab Force.

We got over these difficulties; the British Forces left Kuwait; the Arab Force took over and the Kuwaitis started to build up their own Forces with British help. At Christmas, 1961, after I had left Iraq, British Forces were mobilised on a rumour that Iraq was going to attack, but the rumour proved unfounded. So we came out of the Kuwaiti affair surprisingly well, because Arab interests diverged. When the British Forces went in, the Soviet Ambassador told me with some relish that we were being extremely foolish. We would have all the Arabs against us. He was wrong. That autumn, Mr Zorin argued vigorously in the United Nations that Kuwait could not become a member, since she had no claim to be considered a State. Two years later I had a Kuwaiti colleague in Moscow.

9

ONE of the main slogans of the revolution was the uniting of Arabs and Kurds under the banner of the new régime. Within the first few months Qasim brought back to Iraq the famous Kurdish leader, Mulla Mustapha Barzani, who had been for many years in revolt against the Iraqi Government and had escaped to the Soviet Union in 1947. At the same time, his elder brother, Sheikh Ahmed, the leader of the tribe, was released from detention in Basra. With Mulla Mustapha several hundred Barzanis returned to their old home, where they were resettled by the Government. Mulla Mustapha was given a house in Baghdad and a car, and he, his brother and their families received generous allowances from the Government. Mulla Mustapha now became head of the Kurdish Democratic Party, of leftish political persuasion, with some Communists and a good many fellow-travellers as members. The party pressed for cultural and administrative autonomy for Kurdistan, in accordance with the declarations of successive Iraqi Governments from the time of Iraq's entry into the League of Nations until the early days after the revolution. Early in 1960 the PART party, as it became known, was licensed. The first party manifesto contained a number of extremist passages including attacks on Turkey and Iran. Qasim cut out a good many passages and licensed the party on the basis of his version.

By this time it was already becoming apparent that the Barzanis were not going to settle down peacefully. They were already engaged in sporadic fighting with their neighbours the Zibari and the Baradost. When the party was licensed, I decided to call on Mulla Mustapha, as the leader of the party. I confess I was curious to meet him. Sheikh Ahmed was there and monopolised the conversation, Mulla Mustapha adopting a deferential attitude towards him. Sheikh Ahmed was clearly thinking in terms of the nineteen-twenties. He dilated at length on his relations with various British Governors of Mosul during the mandate and left us in no doubt that he regarded the British Government as having been his principal enemy. Soon after, Mulla Mustapha paid me a return call in order to pass a request from Sheikh Ahmed that I would send him a letter containing an assurance that the British Government would be friendly to the Barzanis. I replied that Sheikh Ahmed did not seem to realise that the mandate was over. The most that I could possibly consider would be to write a letter pointing out that Iraq was an independent State, that we were friendly to all Iraqis including the Barzanis, and that we could have relations with them only through the Iraqi Government. Mulla Mustapha said that he had realised that this would be my reply, but that he had been bound to pass on his brother's request.

I related this incident to the Foreign Minister, in order to prevent misunderstandings. The C.I.D. would have reported my visit. He said that it would be very much against the interests of the British Government to write a letter even in these terms. I realised later that he was right. The fact that any letter had been written could have been used to make trouble. Mulla Mustapha visited me once more and I told him finally that I could write no letter of any kind. He made many complaints against the Iraqi Government, which I did not pass on. He said that the Zibari were attacking the Barzanis and the Assyrians under their protection, burning their houses and carrying off their flocks. The Police did not help the Barzanis who were disgusted with the Government. The British representative at the Baghdad Pact meeting at Ankara told the Iranians and the Turks that I had visited Mulla Mustapha. The Iranians were not concerned. The Turks were suspicious and sent their Ambassador in London to ask why I had gone. They would never have believed that it was only curiosity.

Qasim played off one Kurdish leader against another, giving arms and money to the squabbling tribes on both sides. His familiar policy met with resounding failure. In the autumn of 1960 Mulla Mustapha visited the Soviet Union as the guest of the Soviet Government. On his return, relations between the Barzanis and the Government deteriorated. Tension rose in Kurdistan after the murder of a Kurdish tribal chief, allegedly under Mulla Mustapha's orders. He and Sheikh Ahmed now retired to the mountains. Attempts at a settlement came to nothing. The Government took action against the Kurdish party. By the early summer of 1961 fighting broke out on a wide scale between the Barzanis and the Zibaris. The Barzanis burnt the Zibaris' villages and gained control of most of North-Western Kurdistan. Many tribesmen took refuge in Turkey and Iran and the situation looked like getting out of hand. Qasim reinforced the police and military garrisons, but refused to allow the army to act, hoping apparently to restore peace merely by a show of force. The right-wing Aghas in Eastern Kurdistan joined the Barzanis and by the end of July Qasim was faced with something approaching a full-scale Kurdish revolt from Zakko in the North-

West to Halebja in the East on the Iranian frontier.

The Kurds over-reached themselves. They came down from the mountains, erected road-blocks on the main roads in the plains and threatened the work in progress at the Derbendikhan dam. Numbers of Kurdish policemen and soldiers went over to the rebels. It is possible that Qasim was waiting until he had eliminated the Kurds from the units to be used against the rebels. He decided at last to act and acted with ruthlessness. In about ten days the Kurds were driven back into the hills and rocket-firing and bomber air-craft, making continual sorties, attacked anything moving on the hill roads. For a time, the Police and irregulars in the Zakko-Ahmadiya area in the North-West were in serious difficulties, but the regular Forces soon restored the situation on the roads and in the towns and villages, some of which were totally destroyed by bombing. Sheikh Ahmed made an apparent sub-mission, perhaps to save the Barzani families from the Kurdish irregulars recruited from opposing tribes whom the Government were using against them, but Mulla Mustapha retired to the wild mountain country and continued operations against the Government Forces.

In Baghdad the Government at last admitted the existence of the revolt. Qasim naturally was not going to admit that he was largely to blame. He therefore blamed the British who had spoiled his game in Kuwait. It is possible that he really thought that the British had something to do with it, since it coincided with the awkward moment of the replacement of the British by the Arab Force in Kuwait and with a crisis in the Iraq Petroleum Company's negotiations. The official Press accused the British. Qasim held a Press conference at which he accused the British Embassy of having spent £500,000 to raise the Kurdish revolt, quoting ancient correspondence between British Political Officers and

Mulla Mustapha as evidence of British treasonable connections with him. I remarked to one of Qasim's
staunchest adherents that Mulla Mustapha had been
the guest of the Soviet Government for many years after
that and had recently again visited Moscow. He replied:
'Yes, but he went there as a British agent.' Qasim
exonerated the Soviet Government from any part in
the revolt. This was, I believe, true. A Kurdish revolt
was not in Soviet interests.

I protested; the protest was rejected in relatively mild
terms and the incident was closed. I only found one
person who believed the accusation. One day in the
spring three of us had walked for five hours up a hill in
Kurdistan. The soldier told off to accompany us wisely
lay down under a tree and went to sleep. On our return,
we met some indignant local officials. They said that we
had caused great trouble. The hill was full of wolves,
bears and savage Kurds. They had sent four armed men
after us. We apologised and said that we had met no
wolves or bears and the only Kurds we met had offered
us hospitality for the night. This man, the only one who
would admit to having any doubt that Qasim had
invented the accusation, said that he knew when I had
given the £500,000 to Mulla Mustapha. It was on that
day on the Kurdish mountain.

Qasim explained with pride and with the aid of maps
to his visitors how the revolt had spread over the whole
of the North and how he had crushed it in ten days,
whereas if he had used British methods, it would have
taken him two years. It was an absurd claim. The Arabs,
even Qasim's opponents, thought that the Kurds had
had a good lesson. But Qasim had not put down the
revolt. It continued in the hills and the Kurds had
the sense not to try and defeat the Iraqi army on the
plains again. The Kurds remain unsubdued to this day.

A month after Qasim's denunciation of the British
Embassy, I had to leave Iraq for an operation. The Iraqi

Government reverted to a practice, which they had given up since the early days of the revolution, and, instead of giving me the routine cocktail party in the secondary guest house, gave me a dinner in the principal hall used for receptions. Qasim, his Ministers and senior civil and military officers were there. Qasim was very friendly. He told me how much he appreciated my work as Ambassador and my personal relations with the Government. The £500,000 had disappeared into thin air. Outside the hall, the drivers and a policeman were talking. One driver said: 'I don't understand it. Abdul Karim Qasim says that the British are bad and the British Ambassador a bad man. Now he gives the Ambassador a party.' Another said: 'But you know that Abdul Karim Qasim is a man of the British.' The policeman interjected: 'Without the British, Abdul Karim Qasim is nothing,' and, as the cars were called, he added to my driver: 'Come along, Father of all Embassies.'

So ended my time in Iraq in typically Iraqi fashion. It had been widely believed that Qasim consulted me before every meeting of the Council of Ministers and we had had to work hard to persuade our Nationalist friends that this was nonsense, and that if he had done so, his policy would have made more sense. The Egyptians had put it out that we were supporting Qasim and working with the Communists against Nasser. Qasim had believed that we were concerned in a plot to murder him, and had said that we had raised the Kurdish revolt against him. And so, it was no surprise to hear from an American friend a few months later when my appointment to Moscow was announced, that an Iraqi who had often propounded to him the theory that the British were trying to diminish American influence in Iraq, saw in this clear confirmation that I had been working with the Communists. Some Arabs will believe anything.

Qasim met a violent death in February 1963, being attacked and stormed in his stronghold, the Ministry of Defence. The bloody head was shown on television to 'the people' who he thought had loved him. He had destroyed the Hashemites who might have given stability to Iraq. He gave Iraq nothing but a succession of unstable rulers holding their power by military dictatorship. Iraq has always been a troubled land. It is a difficult country to govern. Perhaps the Arab politician was right when he remarked to me that only two men had ever succeeded in governing Iraq, Hajjaj, the Viceroy of the third Ummayid Khalif, who massacred the people on Friday in the mosques, and Nuri Said, who became old and careless and fell. But with it all, the dust, the heat and the violence, there is hardly any Englishman who has been associated with Iraq, who has not come to feel a real affection for the warm-hearted Iraqi people, among whom my family and I have found some of our most faithful friends.

ADEN 1967

Turning and turning in the widening gyre
The falcon cannot hear the falconer;
Things fall apart; the centre cannot hold;
Mere anarchy is loosed upon the world,
The blood-dimmed tide is loosed, and everywhere
The ceremony of innocence is drowned;
The best lack all conviction, while the worst
Are full of passionate intensity.
. . . somewhere in the sands of the desert
A shape with lion body and the head of a man,
A gaze blank and pitiless as the sun,
Is moving its slow thighs, while all about it
Reel shadows of the indignant desert birds . . .
. . . And what rough beast, its hour come round at last,
Slouches towards Bethlehem to be born?

Yeats: The Second Coming.

ADEN *was a British colony. The States in the hinter-land of South Arabia were not part of the British dominions, but had treaties with the British by which the British gave them protection from external attack on the condition that they did not conduct their own external relations and were bound to accept the Gover-nor of Aden's advice. In February 1959 a Federation of the States of the Western Protectorate was formed and in a few years all the Western States joined it. The three Eastern States which stretched up to the territory of the Sultan of Muscat, did not join and all efforts to make them do so failed. In September 1962 Aden be-came a member of the Federation by a vote heavily weighted in favour of the Government. The British Defence White Paper of 1962 declared that British troops would be based 'permanently' in Aden and the British base was expanded.*

On the day after the vote that Aden should join the Federation, the Imam of the Yemen, who had con-tinually disputed the Yemeni-South Arabian frontier, was overthrown and the new Republic asked for and obtained military support from the Egyptians. Britain did not recognise the new Yemeni régime. Subversive movements in the Protectorate and Aden increased and were supported by the Yemenis and Egyptians. At the end of 1963 British troops were used for some months in support of the Federal army in operations against the dissident Radfan tribesmen in Dhala State. In December the Governor of Aden who was also High Commissioner with the Federation, was wounded and his deputy killed by a bomb. In August 1965 the British Superintendent of Police and Speaker of the Legislative Assembly were murdered. In September 1965 the Aden constitution was suspended and direct rule of the Governor imposed. The dissident political groups built up Forces with which they engaged British and Federal Forces in guerrilla operations, with the avowed aim of ending the British occupation and the rule of the Sultans in the States.

Conferences in London failed to produce a political solution. As early as 1964 it had been agreed that independence should come not later than 1968, with the British base continuing thereafter for an indefinite period, but in February 1966 a new Defence White Paper declared that all British troops would be withdrawn from Aden by 31 December 1968. Nasser, who had agreed with King Feisal at Jedda that he would evacuate the Yemen, now said that he would keep his troops in the Yemen until 1968. The South Arabian problem was transformed by the British decision to withdraw. It was now how to leave behind something which would stand up on its own without the presence of British troops in support.

I

I ARRIVED in Aden on 20 May 1967, to what I and everyone else considered an impossible task. Mr Harold Macmillan had summed it up concisely to me a few days before: 'Poor man,' he said. 'Poor man.' My task was to evacuate the British Forces and their stores in peace, including the large Middle East Headquarters, and, if possible, to leave behind an independent Government which could assure peace and stability in the tiny country of South Arabia, so poor and so ravaged by age-long tribal war and revolution. The British had had such good intentions, but things had gone badly wrong. For a hundred years after Captain Haines had died in a debtor's prison in Bombay, they had occupied Aden as a point essential to imperial communications and had hardly penetrated the interior. The British soldier, passing by on his troopship, gave only a fleeting and incurious glance at Kipling's 'Aden like a barrick stove that's not been lit for years' and the competition-wallah, on his way to his Indian exile, limited his curiosity to an hour's visit to the authentic mermaid and the Indian merchants' stalls at Steamer Point.

Behind the tiny British colony of Aden stretched an inhospitable, barren and mountainous land, with a rugged beauty, enjoying only the rudimentary begin-

nings of economic development, divided into the small
States of the Western Protectorate, one of which was
not even administered and had hardly ever been penetrated by outsiders. In the West and Centre of the Protectorate the States stretched up to the Yemeni border
and were open to infiltration from it. The dominating
figure among the Sultans was the lively black beard,
the Sherif of Baihan, who would sit in his Durbar surrounded by Royalist Sheikhs from over the border, his
eyes bright with enjoyment as he darted his ironies
against British policy, and who, although a Minister
of the Federal Government, had remained for two
years in Baihan without once showing himself in the
Federal capital, responding to requests for advice from
harassed Federal Ministers with oracular and generally
negative replies which by no means helped the resolution of the tangled political problems of South Arabia.
In the Eastern part of the Western Protectorate were
the States dominated by the Aulaqis, less exposed to
incursions of dissidents from the Yemen, providing a
disproportionate number of the army officers under the
influence of old tradition stemming from history and
the recruitment policy of the Aden levies. Further East
were the States of the Eastern Protectorate, the port of
Mukalla pressed against the sea by jagged hills, a hundred miles of waste away from the fertile valley of the
Hadhramaut with its skyscraper villages, the last outpost
before the 'empty quarter', and in the far East the great
desert of Mahra, only occasionally visited until 1963
when in response to the requirements of an American
oil company a solitary Englishman was sent to live
with the tribal council, who received in return a pit-
tance for the few remaining years before independence
from the British who had ignored their existence for
so long.

It was all very romantic in the old way. The national
sport was shooting each other and a modern rifle was

the most prized possession and the only acceptable bribe. The Sultan of Audhali, returning to Aden with me from his village in the hills near the North-Western border, pointed out from the aircraft the ground over which he had so often fought in his youth, saying: 'All this shooting may be new in Aden, but this was how I was brought up.' The old habits persisted and modernisation had not got very far. In one State a man had shot his enemy in the bazaar. The Ruler had ordered that he be immediately shot, without trial, at the place of the murder. This was told to me as an example of the Ruler's justice. Tribal murder was settled by payment of blood-money. Kidnappings across the border were common and could be used as an adjunct to political warfare. A neatly kidnapped broadcaster from San'a Radio was proudly displayed in chains to a member of my staff. Standing on the escarpment near Mukeiras, looking down at that wild, romantic landscape, guarded by dozens of tribesmen dressed like the chorus in *Carmen*, I could understand how the country had captured the hearts of so many British, and how all this rough beauty had sometimes distorted their judgement.

British policy up till the nineteen-fifties may have been, as it has been described, a policy of cynicism and economy, but it had the advantage of avoiding a dangerous involvement in an inhospitable land of warring tribes. In recent years it had changed to what the same author[1] has described as a policy of idealism and cash. It was not only idealism, since Aden, with the increasing danger of subversion from the Yemen and exposed to periodical tribal attacks, needed a protective glacis. In the old days British protection had meant little more than the periodical gift of rifles and ammunition to the sheikhs and the use of the Aden Levies to break up tribal fights which were becoming a nuisance. Now, a small beginning was made with welfare, roads and the

[1] Charles Johnston, *The View from Steamer Point* (1964).

development of the exiguous resources of that barren land. But it was too late to start changing the old ways. Fifty years would have been necessary to make a real impact. Indirect rule with increasing British involvement and responsibility had worked well enough in the Indian States, at a time of imperial growth. But we were on the way out all over the Middle East, having started the process by leaving India, which had treated Aden for so long as an extension of Indian territory and had ignored the existence of the South Arabian hinterland. The policy of developing and modernising the States through the rule of the Sultans was bound to fail.

In due course the Sultans of the Western Protectorate were joined into a Federation of South Arabia. Few of them had had any real authority in their States. They had mostly not been much more than mediators in tribal disputes. Such authority as they had, was further weakened by the removal of power to Al Ittihad, the embryo capital of the Federation outside Aden. The Aden colony itself was brought into the Federation for sound administrative reasons, but by methods which were dubious and widely criticised.[1] Although nominally a member of the Federation and for some purposes subject to its administration, Aden remained a British colony under British jurisdiction until independence. The local Government of Aden made impossible demands and the High Commissioner found it necessary to remove it and suspend the Aden constitution. The High Commissioner thus lost contact with the only political elements in the country of any significance. The Federal Constitution was the best to which agreement could be obtained, but it was deplorable. The States' Rulers were able to hold the dual position of Sultan and Minister. Since the Chairmanship rotated every month, there was no Prime Minister, no leadership and no continuity. Few of the Rulers or their relations

[1] Tom Little, *South Arabia* (1968), pp. 85-88.

who took the positions of some of them on the Federal Council, had the training or experience of administration which they required, and for much of the year the majority of the Council were away in their States or outside the country. After the suspension of the Aden constitution, the Adeni members of the Federal Council were nominated by the High Commissioner. In reality, they represented no one but themselves.

For years, efforts had been made to produce a new constitution which made more sense. When at last a draft emerged, both sides spent months picking at it like a dog worrying a bone. The British lawyers were unhappy because it decided the future of Aden without the agreement of its people, who could hardly be consulted since their elected representatives had been thrown out and there was a guerrilla war on. The lawyers were nervous of being attacked by the churches for passing a clause forbidding proselytisation by missionaries. At last, the constitution was agreed. By that time, it was irrelevant. I refused to take the trouble of reading it. It was obviously never going to come into force. Even if it did, it would never be observed. All these niceties seemed irrelevant to us, since the only question of importance was whether the country would hold together or be submerged in anarchy. On this insecure foundation we had meanwhile superimposed the Middle East Headquarters with its large base and vast collection of equipment, buildings and stores and all the people needed to look after them, for the purpose of underpinning our position in the Gulf, African independence having required us to move it all from Kenya. Once the swimming pools and churches had been built, it was time to leave.

In May 1967 it was a mistake to look back. We probably would have made the same decisions ourselves. Our job was somehow to untie the knot and release ourselves without disaster. The situation was bleak enough. We had declared that we would leave by 1968. Revolution was in full swing. The authority of the Sultans in their little village States in the hills was maintained only by the presence of British troops still in the interior. The Federation was powerless to influence events and lacked credibility. The South Arabian Army and Armed Police, both Forces of the Federal Government, divided within themselves by their tribal origins (the Aulaqis against the rest), and by the growing sympathy of many officers for one or other branch of the nationalist movement, were being hastily expanded to meet the requirements of the plan for the transference of law and order which they were due to take over in a few months' time. Their temper was doubtful, their unity and loyalty precarious.

In Aden the British Forces were able to keep order on the surface by constant patrolling and continual skirmishing against the dissidents. They stopped nearly all the holes by which arms were coming into Aden, but the arms still came in, probably in vehicles of the South Arabian Army and Armed Police, which the Federal Ministers adamantly refused to allow us to search. They were too nervous that their army would turn against them. The whole country was bristling with arms, which were the most valuable currency. In the Protectorate, where everyone was armed, the Sultans collected large stocks and there was a thriving trade to the Royalists in the Yemen, chiefly through Baihan. For years the British had subsidised the Sultans by presents of arms, since this was the cheapest and most acceptable form of subvention. The recipient often never saw the arms. He took the invoice and sold it. No one knew where the arms went after that. Probably they often got into the hands of the dissidents. We stopped this method of subvention; we were at the end of our time and it could be done without difficulty. The Aden Police, still under British control, some of whom were probably engaged in the arms traffic too, had long since been unwilling to oppose the terrorists and were at least partly on the other side. Since we were leaving and they were probably going to have one or other lot of terrorists as their masters, it was not surprising. Wounded terrorists found refuge in the police stations. The British Commissioner of Police turned a blind eye to much of what was happening and limited himself to keeping the Force together. Probably that was all that could be done at that stage. It was too late to clean them out and start again.

The population was intimidated; the administration was rapidly running down, in spite of heroic efforts by British and Arab civil servants against the odds; the streets were unsafe even in the daytime. There were strikes every week, called by one or other of the main underground parties. Labour disputes proliferated; public buildings were burned; oil tanks and pipes were blown up. By this time there were two revolutionary parties, FLOSY, the Front for the Liberation of Southern Yemen, had the allegiance of perhaps half the Adenis, including most of the professional classes. Their principal leaders, Makkawi and Asnag, jockeying for position against each other, tried to lead their party from the rear outside South Arabia, as pensioners of the Egyptians, operating mostly from the Yemen. Makkawi was suffering from the terrible shock of the death of his two sons from a booby-trap in Aden. Flosy's guerrilla force, known as PORF, was almost an Egyptian force, trained, armed and sent clandestinely into South Arabia by the Egyptian Intelligence Service in the Yemen. For the struggle after independence FLOSY were preparing a Liberation Army some twelve hundred strong, which was being trained in Egypt and the Yemen, and Nasser prophesied to a visitor at this time that after independence there would be three days' bloody fighting, succeeded by a revolutionary Government.

The other principal party, the NLF, or National
Liberation Front, which, in spite of Egyptian attempts
to reunite the two parties, were bitterly opposed to
FLOSY, fought on the ground, though they did not
seem, as yet, to have any acknowledged leaders. Such
leaders as there were, had been detained for some time
by Nasser in Egypt, in the interests of FLOSY. The NLF
were mostly young men with a tribal background. They
were strong in the non-Aulaqi States in the West, but
had only few adherents in the Eastern Protectorate,
while the Aulaqi States in between were with FLOSY. In
the army, the NLF were gaining adherents among the
non-Aulaqi officers, though most of the officers were
probably still sitting on the fence, waiting to see who
would come out on top. The NLF had no friends among
the Arab States. Their enemies alleged that they had
Communist affiliations, but of this there was no hard
evidence. But there was evidence that FLOSY had been
in touch with the Communists of Eastern Europe and
were receiving aid from them. The original Nationalist
party, the South Arabian League, known as SAL, were
in decline. They were supported by the Saudis. Their
leaders lived in Saudi Arabia and waited supinely in
comfort in the vain hope that somebody would clear
up the mess and hand the Government to them on a
plate. Some of the Sultans were in touch with them and
intermittently with FLOSY. It was all utterly confused.
There was no clear way ahead.

In March 1967 Mr George Thomson, then Minister
of State in the Foreign Office, had come to Aden to put
the British Government's terms to the Federal Ministers. He had proposed that independence should be
fixed for November 1967, and that the Federal Government should be buttressed for six months after independence by the presence of a Naval Carrier Force
off-shore, able to provide an air deterrent against attack
from the Yemen. The Federal Ministers who wanted

the British to stay as long as possible, refused to accept this offer, and demanded postponement of the date of independence at least until the spring of 1968 and the maintenance of British Land Forces in Aden for an indefinite period to act in their support, with a Defence agreement. They were backed by the right wing of the Conservative party, with whom they were closely in touch. In April they had been told by Lord Shackleton that the British Government had agreed to postpone the date of independence until January 1968, but that the proposals for defence support after independence could not be changed. They neither accepted nor refused the offer.

Meanwhile, the United Nations got in on the act. The Committee on Colonialism, which had a built-in bias against the Colonial Powers, gave birth to the United Nations Mission for South Arabia. It consisted of three gentlemen from Venezuela, Afghanistan and Mali. The mission had visited Aden in April and had been received by a general strike and hostile demonstrations organised by FLOSY. It had refused to deal with the Federal Government, although Federal Ministers knew that before the mission left New York, it had been prepared to meet them in Aden. The members of the mission quarrelled with the High Commissioner and retired in a huff. The visit was a fiasco. The Foreign Secretary calmed them down in a day-long discussion at Dorneywood, but they retired to New York, nursing their outraged dignity and at odds with the British whom they chose to regard as responsible for all their troubles. They then relapsed into inactivity.

South Arabian affairs were now in an impasse. The British Government were being attacked for leaving and did not know how to leave. At home the right championed the Federal Government which hardly inspired much confidence. The left maintained that all we had to do was to get rid of the Federal Government

and hand over to FLOSY. The Federal Government refused to accept independence. The dissidents in South
Arabia only wanted to shoot each other and the British.
The British Government saw only a mess ahead, which
was liable to end up on their heads. Casting around for
something to do, they did what Governments often do
in such circumstances. They unceremoniously changed
the man at the top, as they had changed his predecessor.
The Foreign Secretary pulled me out of the obscurity
of retirement and told me that he was not disposed to
take No for an answer. This was where, on 20 May
1967, I came in.

breakdown from a row with the soldiers'. The glare of Press publicity at home. This was the setting, much like any other 'emergency' in the last days of Empire.

How to grasp the immediate problem quickly? The Federal Government existed and was recognised by the British Government. The British could not legally overturn it nor establish another Government in the Protectorate which was not even British territory. The Adenis waited sceptically to see whether the new face meant a new policy and continued to keep their heads down. A public statement had to be made immediately. Surely, it was better to be definite, right or wrong, than to temporise. We must start by either supporting the Federal Government or throwing it out. We could not throw it out and we had nothing to put in its place; so we must support it. The Foreign Office rightly put in a kink. We 'started from the position' of support for the Federal Government. This was not the end of the matter, since we had serious doubts whether the Federal Government by itself could possibly carry the country through to independence. So the statement went on to say that we looked forward to the establishment of a caretaker Government formed from all parties, and I made it clear that I should be glad to get into touch with the leaders of any party for this purpose.

It was said at this time that British policy was usually 'Divide and rule', but that on this occasion it was 'unite and quit'. We did not expect a positive response from the parties and it did not come, although, with the encouragement of Federal Ministers, we tried by every possible means to get into touch with them. They were manoeuvring against each other. They were afraid of our tricking them, and that, even if we did not trick them, they would be compromised by talking to us. The reactions to the statement were what we expected, derision from the FLOSY Radio in the Yemen, strong criticism from the left-wing at home who were hoping that we should announce the dissolution of the Federal Government; disappointment from those who wanted anything new and thought it was all old stuff, and short-lived satisfaction from the Federal Ministers. Our left-wing critics did not understand that we faced not a strong and coherent nationalist movement, but a prospect of anarchy. If we threw out the Sultans, they would return to their States and stir up trouble for us. There would be a gap in authority and no one with whom we could negotiate. We had to make the best of what we had, while it lasted.

Since we could not negotiate with the Federal Government and the Nationalists, we had to consider whether we could strengthen the Federal Government to a point which would give them a chance of survival by themselves. This had been debated for many months, but it was right to go over the ground again. Could we leave behind British ground troops or a squadron of Hunter aircraft? Could we give the Federal Government a defence agreement which would not put us into an intolerable position? These propositions foundered on the same arguments. A defence agreement would be a guarantee of defence against external attack. But the main danger to the independent Government would almost certainly be internal subversion helped by infiltration across the frontier, not open military attack. Their opponents' plan would be to set up a new revolutionary Government which would then ask the Egyptians to send in troops to support them, on the pattern which had been used in the Yemen. British troops left behind, whether ground troops only or the two battalions required to protect a Royal Air Force squadron, would be in danger of being sucked into a South Arabian civil war, if only in order to protect the perimeter of the airfield which was in mortar range of parts of Aden. If a revolutionary Government took over, the British troops would have to get out ignominiously, probably having to fight their way out.

The situation in Kuwait was very different. There internal subversion was improbable; the danger was of an open Iraqi attack over the desert from Basra. In South Arabia the crux of the matter was the instability of the internal situation and the lack of support for the Federal Government. Even if a defence agreement made military sense, there would be increasing difficulties in carrying it out, now that we had left Africa. We had built the Aden base to protect the Gulf. It would make no sense to build a large base in the Gulf to protect Aden. The military arguments were strong. We could not leave British troops to face the alternative of either being drawn into a civil war with an uncertain outcome or of sitting helplessly and dangerously while the place crumbled round them. A defence agreement would be ineffective against the real danger. We had promised carrier-based air support for six months after independence and were considering strengthening this by stationing V bombers on Masirah island in Muscat territory. No one liked this. There would be demands for air support up country, which would amount to support against internal subversion, since open attack was unlikely. But, if things went wrong, at least the ships could sail away, the aircraft could fly away and at worst we should look rather foolish.

Since we could not help the Federal Government against the dangers which they would most probably face, we could only try and strengthen the Federal Forces sufficiently to enable them to deal with those dangers themselves and thereby give the Federal Government enough confidence to accept the date of independence. Much had been promised. We now offered a squadron of Hunters, four more Jet Provosts, automatic rifles, more 15 pounder guns and armoured cars, and a military mission. The Federal Government realised that they would get no more. 9 January 1968 was fixed as the date for independence, on the basis of the plan to hand over internal security in successive parts of Aden to the South Arabian Army, as soon as the new units were recruited and sufficiently trained, British troops remaining available for a time at each stage to support them if the initial task of dominating the areas taken over should prove to be beyond their powers. The date was fixed for the end of Ramadan, the month of fasting when no one did any work. From Aden we objected to stating the precise date publicly, since we believed that any one of several possible developments would require it to be advanced. We preferred 'by 9 January'; but our recommendation was not accepted, since it was thought that not to be precise would exhibit lack of confidence in the Federal Government's ability to survive.

The civil side was troublesome too. Under the Aden constitution serious offences had to be tried by jury. But no jury would convict a terrorist, for fear of the consequences. A proposal to suspend trial by jury had been refused on grounds of mixed principle and politics. Terrorists could therefore only be detained under the Emergency Regulations. The dissident groups took the line that they could not negotiate until these regulations had been abolished and all detainees released. Even if we complied, there would still be no negotiations. The battling groups had to fight it out first. The British Forces felt that the detainees were too well treated. They had thrown grenades at British troops and were now given television sets. On the other side, the interrogation and detention staff, who had a most difficult task, were subject to attacks by the delegate of the International Red Cross and Amnesty International, which the British authorities in Aden considered to be prejudiced and unfair. Inside the detention centre at Al Mansoura there was periodical trouble, including continual scraps between the FLOSY and NLF detainees.

So we decided to recommend again that the trial of terrorists by jury should be suspended and to see if we could segregate the worst detainees in a separate camp with a tougher régime.

The NLF had been declared an illegal organisation, but not FLOSY. Both were engaged in a guerrilla war against us. We were leaving and it was too late to suppress them. Our declared purpose was to negotiate with them to form a caretaker Government in which all parties would be represented. The NLF objected that they could not negotiate because they were illegal. We had no chance of successfully prosecuting them for being members of an illegal organisation. So we took the logical step and recommended that the proscription should be removed. It was not going to make the slightest practical difference to the British Forces and it put us in a better political position. We also proposed to release thirty of the least bad detainees. We were getting too many of them for the staff to handle properly. And so on 19 June the Foreign Secretary announced the package, the date for independence, the strengthening of the South Arabian Army and Air Force, the promise of off-shore carrier and bomber support, suspension of jury trials of terrorists and the abrogation of the ban on the NLF. I again publicly said that I wanted to get into touch with the leaders of the dissident groups with a view to the formation of a caretaker Government.

During these days, the Arab-Israeli war erupted and was over in a flash. Tension rose in Aden and the Protectorate. There was rioting in the premises of the cotton board in the State East of Aden and a number of British civilians had to be evacuated from up country. There were still about a hundred British up country, mostly with the South Arabian army, and about a hundred more, some with their families, in a vulnerable position, working in the Federal capital outside Aden. Inside Crater, the centre of Aden, the internal security situation rapidly deteriorated. British troops were at this time stationed outside Crater, but patrolled inside in support of the Aden colony's police, who were supposed to be primarily responsible for law and order and had an armed contingent in barracks inside Crater. British troops broke up demonstrations which they had effectively controlled since the visit of the United Nations Mission in April, but still tried to keep off duties which were the responsibility of the police. But the police would not or could not act against the terrorists who, in the atmosphere following the six days' war, were becoming bolder, looting and burning Jewish and foreign property almost without hindrance. Relations between British and Adenis became very strained, particularly during the incident of Nasser's momentary resignation. The British still living in Crater had to move out; the British bankers found it difficult to get to and from their banks in safety and work there, their affairs being complicated by a go-slow of their staff, and British troops had to extend their rôle. The situation was explosive and it only needed one incident to blow everything up. The incident came from a completely irrelevant quarter.

3

O N 20 June the Arab Forces mutinied. This had nothing to do with the Foreign Secretary's statement of the previous day. The new South Arabian Army, which had had its inaugural parade only a few weeks before, had been formed from the Federal Army, itself formed from the old Aden Levies, and the Federal Guard, a Force with a low standard of discipline and training, formed to guard the Sultans and their families in their villages in the interior. At the same time, a South Arabian Armed Police Force was formed from the elements in the Federal Guard not considered good enough to be taken into the new army, and from new recruits. They were to be a gendarmerie, undertaking much the same duties as the old Federal Guard, including the protection of the Federal Capital, which as yet consisted only of offices and houses for Ministers and some officials. The Police of the colony of Aden had an armed branch which was to be amalgamated with the Federal Armed Police on independence, but was, until then, under the direction of the British Police Commissioner and through him of the High Commission. The South Arabian Army and the South Arabian Armed Police were under the command of British Brigadiers lent to the Federal Government.

Some months before, it had become necessary to nominate a senior Arab officer to take command of the army after independence. Against British advice, the Federal Government had appointed Colonel Nasser Buraik, an elderly Aulaqi officer, whom the British considered unsuitable. The Federal Ministers however rejected the advice, since they knew they could count on his loyalty to them. The appointment caused great resentment in the army and the discontent now came to a head. A week or two before, four senior officers, headed by a nephew of the Sherif of Baihan, had written and widely circulated a letter demanding Nasser Buraik's removal. The G.O.C., Aden who was also Inspector General of the Arab army, considered that this insubordination must be treated firmly if discipline was to survive. I supported him by advising the Chairman of the Federal Council to handle the matter himself, firmly but in his own way. The Federal Government suspended the officers.

On 19 June night a movement in the battalion in Little Aden was averted by prompt action. On 20 June morning the cadets in the South Arabian Army's Lake Lines broke out and burnt part of the camp. The soldiers in the camp did not join in, but did not stop the cadets. Soon after, the South Arabian Armed Police in Champion Lines, situated between the airport and British army lines, were told by an unknown trouble maker that the British army were going to attack them A truck-load of British soldiers came along the road, returning from shooting practice. The South Arabian Armed Police opened fire and killed nine of them. They also fired on the British camp and caused casualties. A British detachment cleared part of the lines and took over the ammunition store. At the same time, the South Arabian Armed Police detachment on guard duty in the Federal capital, broke out and demonstrated, breaking windows, banging on doors and tearing down the Federal and British flags. The Chairman of the Federal Council had on his table a letter for signature thanking me for all I had done to help the Federal Government. He escaped to his house and the letter was never signed.

The Federal Ministers gave way. The Minister of Defence ordered the reinstatement of the suspended officers, who were able to restore order in the Lines and, with the help of the Minister of Internal Security, Sultan Saleh of Audhali, at the Federal capital. One battalion of the South Arabian Army outside Aden also became disaffected and marched on Aden. They were met on the road by the reinstated officers and their British Commander and were persuaded to return to their barracks. British troops had shown the utmost restraint in the face of grave provocation and casualties.

The trouble then spread to Crater. It was only some time later that we could get a clear idea of the events of that evening. The centre of the trouble was the Aden Armed Police barracks. The policemen were told by telephone that British troops were going to attack them. They had their families with them in the barrack area. They panicked, broke open the armoury and distributed the arms among themselves and the civil policemen in the station across the road. The Arab Deputy Commissioner warned Aden Brigade that patrols should not go past the barracks. In the meantime, before the Brigade could issue the required orders, three military vehicles went past the barracks. The Armed police and possibly terrorists fired on them. British officers and men were killed. The Deputy Commissioner of Police went to the barracks and succeeded in restoring order. The military Commanders kept British troops out of Crater until the situation should calm down. The bodies were recovered the next day through the Deputy Commissioner of Police. British troops were naturally bitter, but, as Colonel Julian Paget writes, outstanding discipline and leadership were shown.[1]

British troops did not resume patrols inside Crater, but manned road blocks and the hills behind, containing it. The High Commission and Middle East Headquarters were anxious to recover control and resume patrolling in Crater as soon as possible. But the situation was still tense from the six days' war and the events of 20 June. The South Arabian Army and Armed Police were very shaky and might break out again on the slightest provocation. If they did, it would be the end of them. This would have meant our early withdrawal, the victory of the dissidents, the abandonment of most of our stores and, most important, a civil war and the probable massacre of many British still in an exposed position up country or in the Federal capital. Crater was the most sensitive part of Aden. It contained the bulk of the respectable families, Arab and Indian, and many families of members of the South Arabian Army and Police Force. It was considered that the risk of another mutiny if there were to be serious fighting in Crater at that moment, was such that it should be reoccupied by two battalions coming in at night over the hills without using heavy weapons. But the British Brigadiers in command of the South Arabian Army and Police Force declared that even this plan would cause their Forces finally to blow up.

We had to wait another week. Our public position became difficult. We were attacked in the British Press for indecision. We were unable to tell the Press why we did not go back into Crater. Towards the end of the month we were faced with a new difficulty. Although we got a special consignment of currency notes from London, there was not enough currency outside Crater to pay the salaries and meet the demands of the merch-

[1] See the detailed account of these events in Colonel Julian Paget's *Last Post* (1969).

ants at the end of the month. We had to take the risk of sending a convoy into Crater with two British officials, under police guard but without any British army guard, to collect the large sum required from the Currency Board's vaults. There had been a number of robberies by the terrorists who were short of cash, and it was a dangerous operation. We were heartily relieved when it went off without incident.

Some thought that we ought never to go back into Crater, but should let the Arab army take it over, on the ground that the troubles in Aden came from the presence of British troops on the streets and that once they stayed out of the way, everything would be peaceful. We did not accept this thesis. It would have been far too risky. The Khormaksar airport was in mortar range of Crater. We had to keep control of Crater to protect the evacuation. If we put it in charge of the South Arabian Army, we might find them acting against us with the terrorists, or unable to control them. The British civil servants with the Federal Government were rightly concerned for the safety of their British colleagues up country and pressed that we should not go back into Crater, or at least, that if we did, we should give them adequate warning. Even this we could not promise, since surprise was essential.

The Federal Ministers also pressed us to let their army take over and proposed that meanwhile the Aden Armed Police should be reinforced by South Arabian Armed Police. This we could not accept. It would have meant adding to one Force which had mutinied elements of another which had also mutinied. The Aden Armed Police, again quiet and under discipline, were now the only security Force inside Crater. Terrorists were going about openly with their weapons and members of FLOSY and the South Arabian League were kidnapped and murdered by members of the NLF; but there were no security incidents in which British troops were involved except sporadic shooting between terrorists and the soldiers on the surrounding hills. Surprisingly enough, there was no sign of any rebel administration being set up inside Crater. The rebel forces were only intent on killing each other. As time went on, we were increasingly anxious to get back.

After two weeks in all since the day of the mutiny, the Argylls in a most skilful operation went back into Crater and resumed patrolling with hardly a shot fired on either side. They now established themselves permanently in Crater, the first time that British Forces had done this, and quickly secured complete control. The Arab civilians were relieved to see the troops back. They had suffered from the terrorists' comparative free-dom, from the disappearance of the municipal adminis-tration, from rubbish piled up in the streets, from profiteering in foodstuffs and from the ordeal of getting through the searches at check points, if they went out-side to buy the necessities of life. On the day after the reoccupation a military Press conference was inter-preted in the British Press as implying that the High Commissioner had not been consulted about the return to Crater and was at odds with the G.O.C. The Com-mander-in-Chief and I therefore stated jointly that the High Commissioner and the Commander-in-Chief were responsible for policy and the G.O.C. for its execution, that the High Commissioner and the Commander-in-Chief met frequently, sometimes more than once a day, and that we remained in the closest consultation and agreement with each other.

We returned to an uneasy calm. The Federal Govern-ment were too weak to punish their mutineers and accepted a public apology from the instigators of the trouble. We were in a difficulty over the Aden Armed Police. Enquiry now showed that they were probably mainly responsible for the British deaths in Crater. We could not just close the case. We could not pick out the ringleaders. We could not dismiss the whole Force. It was required for normal duties in Crater, and the British Forces did not want to have to take over all police duties. The Federal Government would require the Aden Armed Police after independence. Most important, the British Officers of the South Arabian Police told us that if we punished the Aden Armed Police severely, there would be no more armed police anywhere in the country. We could only temporise. The Chief Justice conducted an official enquiry. The men who had absconded, perhaps the ringleaders, were dismissed, and the matter was left pending until we had gone. There was no other course.

4

It seemed best to keep on stirring the pot. Senior officers from the Arab Army, police and civil service were unanimous that after 20 June the Federal Government had lost the last vestiges of credibility and the loyalty of their Forces. It was now clear that, unless the Federal Government took drastic action, they could not bring the country to independence. Two of the leading Federal Ministers told me that this was what they had been thinking, but that they had not had the courage to say it. We urged them to reform their Government on the lines of the projected constitution and to get some new faces in, to try and regain the loyalty of their Forces and to establish a position from which they could hope to negotiate with the other parties. At present, they were too weak to carry conviction. The main practical advantage of the new constitution was that it provided for a permanent Prime Minister who would choose his Ministers and that no one should act as a State Ruler and Minister at the same time. We recommended that these provisions should be put into effect immediately in advance of the new constitution, through a delegation of powers under the existing constitution, which an obliging Legal Secretary found to be in order.

The Ministers, having heard our views, though hardly taking the matter seriously, appointed Mr Hussain Ali Bayoumi, the Minister of Guidance, a man of great courage, to form a new Government. It was not an easy task. He recruited two of the toughest characters in the Western Protectorate, both of whom had gone over to FLOSY for a time, but who had returned to their old allegiance and had acquired the nickname of 'The Avengers' from their subsequent retaliation against their FLOSY ex-comrades. The Arab Army officers would not take part, but promised support. Prominent Adenis were too frightened to join, but Bayoumi got some candidates who would pass muster and was prepared to add one Federal Minister. At one moment, he had a promise from the leader of the NLF trade union in the British Petroleum refinery. This gentleman suddenly woke up to the realisation that it would do him no good. He therefore gave a grenade to his brother and told him to throw it at Hussain Bayoumi's house. His brother, an old friend of the family, rang the bell and gave it to Bayoumi. They parted with expressions of mutual esteem. Later that evening Bayoumi asked a member of my staff to dispose of the grenade for him, saying that if he kept it in the house, his wife (a most forceful character), would certainly throw it at someone. The Ministers displayed little interest. Some disappeared to their States or abroad. The Chairman said he had not got a quorum, but would put the matter through if I told him to do so. We were not going to get into that position. They had to take the responsibility themselves. Bayoumi took his list to the Council, who rejected it. Bayoumi responded with a vitriolic public attack on his colleagues. Our attempt to strengthen the Federal Government had failed. We could do no more for them.

In Aden political strikes continued, often for no apparent reason. The workers claimed that they should

be paid for non-industrial strike days. In the Port Trust
a series of old disputes came to a head and the management declared a lock-out. Middle East Headquarters
became concerned for their oil supplies and believed
that they would have to requisition the Shell installa-
tion and probably part of the refinery. Unemployment
increased as the Headquarters ran down their staff and
trade diminished. All Jews had been evacuated after
much of their property had been burnt or looted. Every
few days there was some incident of sabotage. The dissident groups were destroying what was to be so soon
their property; but as yet no one believed that the
British were really going to leave. Most of the foreign
community, Indians and Somalis in particular, left for
their country of origin. The atmosphere was still tense
and another mutiny in the South Arabian Forces was
quite likely at any time. Towards the end of June, in
view of the uncertain conditions, we had decided to
accelerate the departure of the military families, who
were due to leave in any case in July, to evacuate the
families of civilian officials and to give strong advice
to other British civilians to send their families home.
Everyone co-operated. It could not be seriously disputed that it was the right decision.

The United Nations Mission now began to stir again.
They showed no signs of wanting to return to Aden;
once was enough for them. They made overtures to
FLOSY and it seemed possible that they would declare
FLOSY the rightful heir, although its leaders dared not
appear openly in the streets of Aden. The Mission having asked to see me, I told them fully and frankly what
it all looked like in Aden. They were about to open up
shop in Geneva. They agreed to see the 'representatives
of the Western and Eastern States', a formula which
would not require them to recognise the Federal
Government's existence. I urged them not to ignore
the NLF, which was an important piece on the

board. We parted amicably. I did not see them again.

We advised the Federal Ministers and the Rulers of the Eastern States to send delegations. The Eastern States' Rulers decided to go themselves. Practically all the Federal Ministers wanted to go. Since the Lahej State was already showing signs of crumbling, I wrote to the Chairman of the Council advising them to leave a strong team behind. In the event, there were only two Sultans from the Western States in Geneva, but a large delegation went and only three Ministers stayed in Aden, the Sultan of Lahej among them. The formula agreed in New York did not cover the Adeni Ministers, who were not going to be left out. So two of them went as representatives of a party which had been formed as a moderate party in earlier and more promising days, but which had now lost whatever support it had formerly enjoyed. The third Adeni Minister declared himself to represent an Arab political movement in Beirut which had probably never heard of him. One Minister went off to Cairo on the way to Geneva and made contact with the Egyptian Government and FLOSY. It was all getting properly mixed up. The United Nations Mission sat disconsolately in Geneva seeing no one except Lord Shackleton, the Federal Ministers whom they pretended did not exist as such, and the Rulers of the Eastern States, one a young man straight from an English school, one a tribal leader from the Hadhramaut and one a member of the tribal council of Mahra, straight from the desert. The mission saw FLOSY on the way home, having to run after them to Egypt, but the NLF refused to go near them. Their attempt to settle the future of South Arabia from outside the country had failed, as all such attempts had failed before.

The distant desert States of the Eastern Aden Protectorate had never come into the Federation. The British Government had tried to push them in by threatening to give aid after independence only through the independent Federal Government. The Eastern Rulers, very reasonably, saw no reason why they should merge with so shaky an enterprise as the Federation. They were waiting to see what would happen. Everyone else in South Arabia wanted the British to hand over the Eastern States on independence, on the ground that they were part of the country, as indeed they were, and suspected that the British would try and keep them as a base for their nefarious activities after they had given up the Western States and Aden. We could not oblige them. The States were not British territory and British protection was to be unilaterally withdrawn from them all when the country became an independent State.

There were other complications. The British financed and directed a sort of 'beau geste' Force, the Hadhrami Beduin Legion, which, apart from murdering its British officers every now and again, roamed round those deserts knocking off any tribe that caused trouble. They kept the peace effectively and preserved the Eastern frontier of the Federation. The solitary British officer, who commanded them, dressed in the approved Anglo-Arab style, lived with his Force at its headquarters a few miles outside the port of Mukalla and could be held as a hostage at any time that we did something which the Legion did not like. We also subsidised State Forces in two of the three Eastern States, which guarded the Rulers, their Treasuries and jails, but were not much good for anything else.

Security in Mukalla was uncertain. The Political Agent, his wife and his staff lived in the Residency opposite the Palace, guarded by a few S.A.S. men. We sent a detachment with helicopters to the old R.A.F. staging post at Riyan, fifteen miles away, but Mukalla could only be approached by land through defiles from the heights of which ambushes could easily be mounted. In the period of tension after the June war, there were demonstrations against the Residency. A detachment of the Beduin Legion fired over the heads of the crowd so that the bullets landed on the Palace opposite. The State Forces guarding the Palace fired back. The S.A.S. wireless operators in the Residency tower sat on the floor to avoid the bullets and the Political Agent's wife proudly displayed the wall of her bedroom spattered with bullet holes. There was a British Political Agent and Police Officer a hundred miles over the waste in the Hadramut at Saiyun, from which we could evacuate them by helicopter. The man in Mahra was safe in the hands of his Beduin friends. We knew we could not keep British in the Eastern States after October, but did not want to take them out before we had to, since that would show that we were abandoning the Rulers and everything might then go to pieces. It was going to be bad enough anyway when we had to get out.

One proposal was that we should disband the Legion. That was not so easy. Their rifles would be worth more than their gratuities and they would merely disperse and turn into bands of roving gangsters, with their military training to help them. This would mean anarchy in the Eastern States and greatly weaken the Eastern border of the Federation, opening it to more incursions from the Yemen and by the Saudi tribes. The only arrangement we could think of was that the British Government should continue their military aid, paying completely for the Legion and subsidising the State Forces for three years after independence, on condition that the States created a joint council to run the legion and made an agreement with the Federal Government on co-operation between the Legion and the South Arabian Army. We were sceptical whether the three States would ever co-operate with one another to that extent and knew that we should be accused of removing the only inducement to the Eastern States to enter the Federation. As a gesture to the old policy we maintained the previous decision that the civil aid would only come through the Federation, but this was a very small proportion of the total. No one liked having to promise the money. The United Nations Mission were highly suspicious of what we were up to. The Eastern Rulers made an agreement in principle to run the Legion together, but then diverged into discussing a federation of their own, which obviously would never come off. We stuck to our point. We could not disband the Legion. We could not just stop paying it. We could not blame the Eastern Rulers for not rushing into the arms of the rickety Western Federation.

5

BRITISH Forces had been in the Western States as a backing for the South Arabian Army until 30 June. We had no responsibility under the Treaties which we were unilaterally abrogating on independence, except to support the Rulers against attack from outside the country. Internal security was the Rulers' responsibility, although in our interests we had reserved the right to intervene in the States on our own initiative. But the presence of the British Forces had bolstered up the internal security of the States, and they had been extensively engaged in operations such as the Radfan campaign against dissidents. Up till the end, there were parties of Sappers in the Protectorate, making roads and minor irrigation works and getting blown up by mines or ambushed for their pains. One of them had said to a Sheikh that they surely did not need a guard when they were digging a well for the people. 'You don't know these people,' was the reply.

At the end of June, the first stage of the evacuation plan was complete. British Forces were withdrawn into Aden and were to be withdrawn progressively from successive parts of Aden until the final evacuation. This was the only feasible way of getting out in an orderly way. By August, it was generally known that we had left the Protectorate and the Central and Western States crumbled within a week or two, the NLF mostly taking over, though in the large State of Lahej, between Aden and the Yemeni frontier, the NLF and FLOSY were about evenly balanced. The nephew of the Sultan of Lahej, who was a senior officer in the South Arabian Police, was sent to Lahej to restore order. Even he, though so closely connected with the ruling families, announced before he left that he was not going for the purpose of restoring Sultanic rule. He just managed, with the help of the senior officers of the South Arabian Army, to arrest some of the dissident leaders and then had to escape from the country himself. The prisoners were transferred to the prison of the Fadhli Sultanate East of Aden, from which they and all the State prisoners, including a notorious multiple murderer, were released a few days later by the Sultan before he fled. The Audhali State where I had so recently been with its Sultan, fell in a moment. The Sultan was ill in London. His two Deputies fled. We could not turn round and send British Ground Forces back into the States. It would have been fatal to get involved in a major campaign at this stage of the evacuation. We should have had to bring large reinforcements from England and postpone the evacuation indefinitely, and as soon as we retired, the Sultans would fall again. We had to stick to the decision to withdraw. We were not going to create a little Vietnam.

We had twice given air support to the South Arabian Army during these events at their request, since their Air Force was still in the making, once against a FLOSY attack on a customs post on the Yemen frontier, led by one of its leaders with the other lurking in the background, and once against a fort flying the NLF flag. But the Sultans had lost the support of their army and since the mutiny the British Commander could no longer rely on his orders being carried out. He had to

persuade and senior officers made the decisions in committee. He became a sort of senior sheikh, mediating
between the factions, pressing them to take sensible
political action and knocking their heads together when
they became too excited or looked like getting involved
in faction fighting. They respected him and listened
to him; but he could not make them do what they did
not want. It was all very precarious, but we had no
option. We had to keep close to the Arab Army and try
and keep it together and support it, since it was
the only element of stability in the country, highly
unstable though it was, and we needed it to cover our
evacuation.

The Defence Minister, who was also Sultan of Lahej,
came to us with an official who had fled from another
State, to ask us to bomb two villages in the State. I said
we would require a request from the South Arabian
Army. The Defence Minister argued that it was subject
to his orders. We replied that he could order the army
to make the request. It was not forthcoming. To have
bombed villages otherwise than in support of the army
would have been dangerous and ineffective.

In several States large quantities of arms, including
rocket launchers, bazookas and mortars, were picked
up by the NLF guerrillas. This was an added hazard to
the evacuation. During these events, much of the South
Arabian Armed Police disintegrated and many men disappeared with their rifles. They had to be rounded up
again when the South Arabian Army recovered control.
I learnt afterwards that two of the most prominent Sultans had been subsidising the NLF. Little good it did
them. With the help of the Arab army, the Sultans'
families were brought down from their States and
evacuated by air to Saudi Arabia, where they wanted to
go. King Feisal received them, but was not pleased. One
minister, himself a Sultan, was caught by the NLF in
his village and put under house arrest. So ended the

Sultans and with them the plan to build on insecure foundations a Federation of South Arabia.

Even before the Sultans fell, the Arab army had been discussing among themselves and with one Minister a plan to take over power from the Ministers, who were obviously not going to last much longer. We told them that if they took over, we would deal with them as a Government, but we were sceptical whether they could do so, since they were disunited themselves. And so it turned out. They postponed their plans. The Minister with whom they had been discussing their ideas, published an appeal to the army to take over, which made it finally certain that nothing would happen. They could not be seen to be taking power at the request of a Federal Minister.

The Federal Government soon finally collapsed and the last remaining Ministers dispersed. The Sultans managed to survive a little longer only in the Aulaqi States to the North-East of Aden, with the help of FLOSY. Hussain Ali Bayoumi, the Minister who had tried to form a new Government, courageously came back to Aden from Geneva and resumed his position as Minister of Guidance; but he was warned off the Federal capital by the NLF and finally left the country. The young Ruler of the Wahidi State returned and asked the R.A.F. to take him to his capital. Without instructions, a British officer working with the South Arabian Army and a sergeant pilot took him there in a helicopter. They landed in the middle of the town. The two British were killed. The young Ruler was taken away. There was nothing we could do. We had left all that country and could not go back.

Owing to the radical change in the political situation, the Arab army were no longer in a position to accept the backing of British Forces, once they had taken over internal security in different parts of Aden. The plans for raising the last units had been advanced. The previous time-table for the progressive hand-over in Aden no longer fitted the situation. It was obvious that after what had happened, we had better be out as soon as we could get ready and that for that purpose we should finish getting our stores out as soon as possible. We needed a more flexible time-table. We therefore recommended to the Foreign Office that we should say publicly that on a further appraisal of our progress in the evacuation, we expected to advance the date of independence. This would get us off the hook of the precise January date. They did not agree to a public announcement of a change in the evacuation dates which it was felt would hasten disintegration, but gave us the authority to complete the removal of stores by early November and to plan to get out by 20 November. This leaked as we knew and had warned London that it would. So we were able to put the dissidents on notice that they could not go on indulging in the luxury of shooting us and avoiding responsibility for much longer.

We had to continue the absurdly difficult task of trying to find a political group able and willing to take responsibility. They were still unwilling to come out into the open. We now faced that situation which we had tried to avoid. There was no Government, only an army and civil servants with no authority over them. There was serious danger of anarchy. The British and Arab civil servants from the Federal capital urged an immediate British move. Everyone was looking to us. The NLF were not far from Aden and might at any moment take over the Federal capital. The senior officers of the Arab army demanded a statement from us recognising the new position. We had to keep the initiative.

With the Foreign Secretary's agreement therefore and the strong support of Middle East Headquarters and British Commanders who were in close touch with

the local situation, I made a public statement on 5
September that the Federal Government was no longer
functioning and that we recognised the political groups
as representing the people of the country and would
negotiate with them. We stated no preference for the
group which looked like coming out on top, the NLF,
since the army was still split between the political
groups and FLOSY was not yet dead, but we added
that since Qahtan as Sha'abi, who had now emerged
as the NLF leader, had told a correspondent that he
was ready to talk to us, we should be glad to accept the
offer. This had needed discussion in London, since it
was a major political step and officials had been concerned about possible Saudi reactions. We were grateful to the Foreign Secretary who had backed us through
all our crises and had an imaginative grasp of the situation. Lord Shackleton told the United Nations mission
what we were doing. Their reaction was odd. Two of
the members took it reasonably, though they did not
like anyone else butting in on what they considered
their preserve. The third member was violently hostile
and persuaded his colleagues to break off the talks with
Lord Shackleton. We could only speculate why.

On the evening on which I made my statement, the
senior Arab officers from both factions came to see me.
The FLOSY faction accused me of partisanship with
the NLF, because the Arabic version of my statement
used the word 'qaumi' for nationalist and not 'watani'.
The word 'qaumi' was used generally for 'nationalist'
all over the Arab world, but in South Arabia was more
often used for the NLF. I responded by attacking them
for not uniting to save their country. I refused to alter
the word, but agreed to make it clear on the radio that
I was ready to have talks with all the political groups.
They calmed down. After a little prompting by their
Commander, the army responded to my statement with
a public declaration supporting it, urging the groups

to come forward and talk to me and promising their support to any group which did so. At the same time, they helped to hold the position by taking control, if not very effectively, of the approaches to Aden, including the Federal capital, presumably in agreement with the NLF, which still kept away from it.

The most welcome consequence of our statement was the virtual cessation of attacks against British servicemen and civilians for about six weeks, a form of undeclared truce, which we were surprised lasted as long as it did in the face of British Press correspondents' questions to the NLF leaders whether there was one. The NLF leaders who had come out into the open in a village not far from Aden, did not respond to our offer and admitted privately that they did not dare being seen talking to us. We deduced that they did not feel strong enough to take responsibility while the army was still divided and they had not got control of the Aulaqi States which were so heavily represented among the army officers. The only overture from FLOSY had been an approach to the British Government outside South Arabia by one of the main leaders, apparently without the knowledge of the other. As his idea was that we should put FLOSY into a dominant position with their own private army to protect them and knock out the rest, nothing came of it.

The FLOSY line was now that we were in with the NLF and the Sultans in exile put it about that I had made a deal with the NLF to send them all to Geneva, so that the NLF could conduct their revolution in peace. I have no doubt that this story greatly enhanced my reputation in the Middle East, but it was of course wholly untrue. Despite all our efforts to get into touch with the NLF, we had no communication with them, even indirect, until the last three weeks before independence. Our efforts to get the Federal Government to leave a strong team behind in Aden had met with little response, but in any case the Sultans were by that time so weak that even if the few Sultans at Geneva and those who had dispersed elsewhere had been in their States and all the members of the Federal Government in the Federal capital, the course of events would have been much the same.

The political situation remained static throughout September. The army, conscious of its own internal divisions, pressed the two sides to come to terms with each other. At last, at the end of the month, the two groups agreed to meet in Cairo. We issued a statement that we would negotiate with any group set up after the conference, a phrase carefully worded by Foreign Office officials to answer Saudi objections that we were ignoring their ineffective protégés, the South Arabian League, and to provide for the probable contingency that there would be no agreement in Cairo. We added that we would soon be ready to leave and that the groups should come to a quick decision. This statement had no effect whatsoever.

Up to the issue of the statement of 5 September, the fighting in Aden had continued with increasing intensity and some British casualties. Three-inch mortar shells fired at Government House fell wide of the mark. On the next day the guerrillas fired two-inch mortars at Middle East Headquarters, thus preserving the protocol. The most distressing feature of the Aden fighting, at this time and later, were the deaths of a number of civilians and of soldiers off duty, nearly all shot in the back of the neck by a sniper who was never captured. The Aden streets became progressively more unsafe. Special military guards had to be provided for the British banks which had moved out of Crater, and in the shopping centres at fixed times. No woman was directly attacked, but this could not be relied on. British women had been killed before my time. All British civilians were withdrawn into safe areas.

The groups' guerrillas fought the British and each other. But in some respects the situation looked a little brighter. At last the NLF seemed to be beginning to realise that they should not destroy their own property, and sabotage gradually diminished. The industrial situation suddenly improved for no obvious reason. In Aden, as we said, things went from good to worse and from bad to better. Middle East Headquarters found that by various devices, including the use of a small specialised products carrier caught on the wrong side of the Suez Canal when it was closed, it would be possible to avoid requisitioning oil installations. People seemed to be tired of strikes and even the Port Trust achieved a settlement of its labour disputes, though few ships came in after the closing of the Suez Canal. We had continued our preparation of cases against terrorists for trial without jury, but it became apparent in the end that the difficulties of arranging these trials were too great and they were abandoned. In any case, after recent events, it was now certain that the punishment would be no more than a few months' imprisonment before release at independence. Similarly, the proposal to institute a more severe régime for the worst detainees failed, since it would not now be possible to establish the new detention camp in an area to be handed over to the South Arabian Army. Practically nothing of the British Government's statement of 19 June was left.

After the fall of the Sultans we had to withdraw all British working outside Aden. Even the British officials in the Federal capital, a few miles outside Aden, were in too exposed a position. One had been ambushed and killed on the road and it was expected that the place would be attacked and looted. We had to make sure that all the political papers were removed from the High Commission's political liaison office there. A little farce crept in. The trouble was, they said, that the combination lock was stuck and only the girls, who had been evacuated, could open the safe. Miraculously, an amateur safe-opener appeared and did the trick.

We could no longer leave the British in the Eastern States, as soon as the intervening territory became uncertain and communications for helicopters became unsafe. The R.A.F. staging post at Riyan, which had been in existence for forty years, was abandoned. There were no more British in the East of South Arabia. The Eastern Sultans returned to Mukalla by ship and were met by the NLF. They refused to leave the ship and retired to Saudi Arabia. We were sorry that it had turned out this way, though the Eastern Sultans were perhaps lucky that they were not there when the NLF took over. The NLF were now in command of at least part of the Eastern Protectorate and we had no alternative, if peace was to be maintained in the East until we left, to continue to pay the Hadrami Beduin Legion while they adjusted themselves to serving the new régime. In this they seemed to have no difficulty, and, although our subsidy ceased on independence, money was found to keep them in existence thereafter.

On 12 September we started to hand over internal security in the Aden area with the transfer of responsibility for Little Aden with the British Petroleum Company's refinery to the South Arabian Army. Our action was justified. There was no more trouble there. Twelve days later, we handed over the suburbs of Sheikh Othman and Mansoura, where British troops had had to cope with fierce factional fighting. This was an awkward situation, since they were responsible for internal security but did not want to get involved. It broke out again after the Arab army took over, but they managed to stop it by establishing tripartite committees of themselves and of FLOSY and the NLF. British troops had now withdrawn from half Aden and there was no longer any doubt in Arab minds that we were really going. Since the main detention camp was in the area handed over, we released all the detainees except a hard core of thirty, who were kept in an area under our control until we finally left. We heard with some satisfaction that the International Red Cross which had hitherto concentrated on us, had told their representative to start investigating the detention camps which had now been established by the NLF to house their captured opponents.

Meanwhile, FLOSY had tried to make a come-back in the Western States with reinforcements from the Yemen, but had been beaten back by the NLF, who had consolidated their hold on the Western and Central States of the Western Protectorate. The situation was now moving further in favour of the NLF as a result of the Egyptian-Saudi agreement reached at the Arab Leaders' conference in Khartoum, under which Egyptian troops were to evacuate the Yemen. After all that had happened, it was ironical that we and the Egyptians should be leaving South Arabia at the same time. The Egyptians began their withdrawal and FLOSY and their guerrilla arm PORF lost their bases and sources of supply. Up in the North-West the old Sherif of Baihan had sat tight, but now, warned by what was happening elsewhere, he drove off by the desert route to Saudi Arabia with a large following of his Sheikhs. The Sheikhs came back later, without the Sherif. On his departure, the local NLF took over, aided privately by members of the South Arabian battalion stationed in Baihan.

The Baihan-Yemeni frontier became a point of tension. The Sherif, naturally furious with the British, was hoping to return to his State with the support of the Yemeni Royalists at Harib, just over the border, and of the Saudis. He was profuse in his accusations that the South Arabian Army, still nominally commanded by a British officer, had overturned his Government and looted his property. There were suspicious movements over the frontier. We therefore warned the Sherif and the Saudis that our policy was to support the South Arabian Army and that in accordance with our previous practice we would support them with the R.A.F. against any attack from over the frontier. The Sherif kept quiet, but the Arab army battalion at Baihan again became involved when they helped the Republican Sheikh of Harib, who, doubtless with the Sherif's help, had been dispossessed by the Royalists, to recover his lost village. They denied it, of course, but there was not much doubt about it, since it was in the interest of any-one holding Baihan to have a friend in the strong point over the border. So we had come to threaten the use of British aircraft against an attempt by a man who was still nominally under British protection, to recover his State by attacking from across the frontier the rebels who had usurped his power with the aid of a battalion which we were helping to pay and arm and which was still nominally under British command. We were right to do so. We could not compromise our main objective to leave in peace and leave the country at peace.

6

THE NLF and FLOSY, the principal contenders for power, met at last in Cairo in the second week of October and settled down in a leisurely way to private talks and evening sessions in the night-clubs. Each party wanted two-thirds of the posts in the Government. Nothing was heard in Aden and everyone was sceptical whether there would be any agreement in Cairo. The Egyptians commented ruefully that we were now to the left of them in South Arabia. They were in a weak position in dealing with the Saudis who were compensating them for the closure of the Suez canal, and they had therefore at least to pretend to agree to the attempts by the Arab League under Saudi instigation to form a South Arabian Government with five members each for FLOSY and the NLF and three each for the South Arabian League and the Sultans, whom the Saudis in any case wanted off their hands. These efforts came to nothing since the NLF were by now confident that they would win and saw no reason why they should make concessions to anyone else and since the FLOSY leaders would only feel safe in Aden if they had a dominant position in the Government. During the month we continued pressing for a settlement in Cairo and tried to get Nasser to intervene and force an agreement, or at least to get the groups to send a joint party to Aden to stop the factional fighting. Presumably Nasser had no influence on them. The most we got was a statement on Cairo radio that an agreement had been reached and would be announced in a few days, a statement which no one believed.

Towards the end of the month we considered it time again to put the groups on notice that we were not going to stay indefinitely while they continued their squabbles and fighting. The removal of stores had gone well and we were now in a position to leave without abandoning anything we wanted to take away. The Foreign Secretary therefore, on my recommendation, announced on 2 November that British troops would in any case leave by the end of November. This was a difficult decision for him to take, since it amounted to saying that, if necessary, we would leave the country in chaos. But we had to put on the pressure if we were ever going to see something emerge in South Arabia and we had now gone so far in our evacuation that we could not stay much longer without unacceptable risks. With every stage of the evacuation we became weaker. Every week that we stayed after the removal of our stores, now to be completed early in November, was an added risk of British casualties without any purpose. Evacuation must mean independence. I was not going to put myself into the position of sitting in Government House without the backing of British troops. Already the authority of Government in Aden was almost completely eroded. The NLF were collecting dues and exercising increasing authority. It was high time we left, whatever we left behind.

Tension between the groups in Aden now increased. FLOSY still had substantial support in the town and knew that this was their last chance. Their guerrillas, PORF, would not get any more supplies from the

Egyptians in the Yemen. The groups began fighting each other again. They renewed their attacks on the British in order to prove their Nationalist credentials. This angered me. It was more pointless than ever. PORF, reputedly against the advice of the NLF, took on the Argylls in Crater, but quickly gave up after severe casualties. The murderer started again and, before the end, had added to his victims a Danish sea captain, a German television correspondent, a young member of my staff who was particularly friendly to the Arabs and, very nearly, an elderly Scot who was shot in the stomach while walking from his bedroom in the annexe of the Crescent Hotel to the dining room. The correspondents sensibly retired from the hotel, now manifestly unsafe, to a lodging behind the British wire. British working for the Federal Government in and around Aden found it increasingly dangerous to carry on their jobs, but carried on with stout hearts, though with no prospects for the future.

Every week or two we were faced with a situation tending to split the Arab army and it was only the patience, courage, firmness and tact of Brigadier Dye, the British Commander, which kept the Arab army in being. An Aulaqi Battalion Commander published a statement that he would take on all-comers, especially the British and the NLF. The British Commander had to intervene at considerable personal risk to settle a quarrel between the factions in a distant army camp. The trouble came to a head when one of the senior officers of the South Arabian Armed Police, which no longer had a British Commander, organised on behalf of the NLF an armed column which set off to the East, gathering tribal reinforcements on the way, ostensibly to round up armed policemen who had deserted and their arms, but really to help complete the subjugation of the Aulaqi States. The senior Aulaqi officers came to me in a state of great excitement and said that if I did not stop the column, they would have to desert and go home to protect their families.

A FLOSY Press conference was held, attended by officers in uniform, at which the British and the NLF were accused of being in league against the Aulaqis. We were accused of having handed over two thousand Mauser rifles to arm the column. These were contraband rifles which had been found in the port under false labels. The Federal Ministers had wanted them to sell. We had held on to them and were breaking them up to dump in the sea, when the Commissioner of the Aden Police, now an Arab, who had also succeeded to the command of the South Arabian Police, asked for them for his Police work. We gave them to him on the strict injunction that he would not use them for any other purpose while we were still in Aden. We now had to ask for them back to kill this story. He returned them all in perfect repair. Before we left we gave them to the Commander of the battalion which was looking after the refinery.

As the column moved on, watched every day by the R.A.F., the situation grew more tense. I therefore summoned the senior officers of both factions and delivered a formal lecture to them on their duties to their country and to their own future. They admitted the truth of what I had said. After two days of Arab discussion conducted by my Counsellor, Mr Burroughs, they calmed down and a compromise was reached. The column was kept out of Aulaqi territory and the army remained intact. We wondered whether we could keep it together until we left. In a few weeks the remnants of the opposition to the NLF in the Aulaqi States collapsed and the NLF finally took over these States after a battle in which one Sheikh fired off all his heavy ammunition at his opponents' houses before he left. The battle in the States was at least adjourned until after independence.

At the beginning of November, a fierce battle raged between the factions in the suburb of Sheikh Othman. There was now no hope of conciliation. The Arab army were unable to control it. On 7 November the Arab army declared for the NLF. This was a crucial decision. It was now clear who was winning. So only a few Aulaqi officers resigned and the army did not split as we had feared it would. In a few days the remaining FLOSY and PORF fighters were defeated and either captured or dispersed by the Arab army and the NLF acting together. They also acted together in publicly asking for recognition by the British Government. We recommended that we should state that we recognised that the NLF was in control and was the body to which authority should be transferred.

There was a pause while British Ministers considered the next move. British and foreign Press correspondents now in Aden in large numbers for the final withdrawal, could not understand why we did not recognise the obvious. It was like a game of snakes and ladders when you land on a snake just short of the post. There was obviously some difficulty at the other end. The reply came. Ministers did not agree. The way they looked at it in London was that they must not appear to be putting the NLF into power, nor were they prepared to repeat that we would negotiate with the NLF in answer to a declaration at a Press Conference, as we had at the beginning of September. The NLF must now ask us directly for negotiations. We did not see it in this way. It was by this time obvious that we only had the choice to hand over to the NLF or to nobody. We were lucky in at last finding someone to whom we might be able to hand over in peace. Perhaps the Foreign Office were right in thinking that the NLF wanted negotiations quite as much as we did. But they might suspect that we were stalling and that they were not going to get any money out of us and in that case,

with the Arab army now their allies, they were quite
capable of turning round and fighting us out of Aden
in the most difficult final phase of the evacuation. South
Arabians had an unrivalled appetite for self-destruction.
If they asked for negotiations and we agreed, we should
be putting them into power anyway. What was the use
of standing on our dignity and taking a fresh risk for a
point which seemed to us to have no practical
importance? Could it be that they thought in London
that it was better that we should get out as best we
could without negotiations and without paying anything? It was one of those situations which look
completely different at either end.

We had no direct contact with the NLF leaders, but
by this time we were negotiating through senior Arab
officers who were in close touch with them. I told the
officers, with a pardonable stretching of the truth, that
it was against our constitutional practice to recognise
political bodies in these circumstances and that recognition would be given by the act of negotiation. They
should therefore propose a negotiation. My argument
was so thin that we thought that they would be
suspicious and refuse to make another move. A telegram
that I was on my way home with the Commander-in-
Chief for discussion was already drafted. The delegation
turned up again with the required message. I tore up
the telegram.

It was now 11 November. Negotiations were to be
held in Geneva, Lord Shackleton leading for the
British. Their prospects were highly uncertain. Our
stores were all away. There was nothing to keep us. It
was better for us to go as soon as possible. We proposed
to the NLF through the army that the negotiations
should begin on 16 November and that we should
leave on the twenty-second. The army agreed; the NLF
did not. Their representatives could not reach Geneva
until the twentieth; would we please stay as long as

possible? We had to balance the risk of staying on another ten days during which the atmosphere might suddenly go sour and the suspicion that they would prefer to negotiate while there were still hostages on the ground, against the possibility that if we insisted on the earlier date, they would refuse to negotiate, suspecting that we were trying to leave without making any agreement with them. We had said that we would leave by the end of November. On balance, it seemed wiser to stay a few days longer. We fixed 30 November as independence day.

There had been one tiresome side issue, the islands. Kamaran, an old quarantine station three miles off the coast of Yemen and five hundred miles from South Arabia, had fallen into our lap on the break-up of the Turkish Empire. We had remained in possession without claiming sovereignty. Perim, at the mouth of the Red Sea, a mile or two off the Yemen coast but not far from South Arabian territory, was British territory and was useful for its navigational light. The Kuria Murias, hundreds of miles up the South Arabian coast, opposite Muscat, had been Muscat territory until a hundred years before, when a British naval captain, observing guano on the shore, had obtained an allegedly free gift of the islands to Queen Victoria. Kamaran had a population of a few thousand and under the indulgent eye of a British official, subsisted mainly on selling duty-free liquor to passing ships and Egyptian officers on the mainland. Perim had a few hundred fishermen and the lighthouse-keepers on it, with Arab officials under the Aden Government. Seventy-five illiterate fishermen inhabited the Kuria Murias, which had no officials, British or Arab, on them and were visited once a year. The guano had been exhausted in a few years and the islands had been of no use to us since. The other South Arabian island, Socotra, presented no trouble. It was recognised as attached to the Eastern State of Mahra.

All South Arabian parties demanded that we hand over the islands on independence. The Foreign Secretary had committed himself in Parliament to putting to the United Nations the proposition that Perim should be internationalised, to prevent its being used to blockade the southern entrance of the Red Sea, which, incidentally, could be as easily blockaded from the Yemen coast a few miles away. The Minister of State had promised Parliament to consult the wishes of the inhabitants of all the islands. The Foreign Office sent long and involved telegrams. We proposed to them that we should hand over Perim to South Arabia, that, like the snark, we should softly and silently vanish away from Kamaran without making any attempt to defend it from Yemeni attack or saying anything about its future status, and that we should tell the South Arabians that we regarded the Kuria Murias as having nothing to do with South Arabia and as reverting to the sovereignty of Muscat. We conducted our referendum on Perim one afternoon and it passed peacefully to South Arabia. The people of Kamaran also, now that the Sultans had fallen, declared for South Arabia and the Yemeni Republicans, who were in contact with the NLF, did not dispute the succession. On the Kuria Murias we conducted a referendum during the annual visit and they opted for Muscat. There could be no agreement with the South Arabians on them.

Lord Shackleton, who had so willingly and ably pursued our interests outside South Arabia, met the NLF negotiators in Geneva on 22 November. The negotiations were not easy. At one moment most members of his delegation believed that they would break down. The NLF wanted us to guarantee the amount which we had promised the Sultans for the first three years of independence. There were the Kuria Murias. Since no agreement had been reached a few days before we were due to leave, we sent off most of the staff earmarked for the new Embassy and finally sent home all the remaining British civil servants working with the Federation and the Aden Government. We were ready to remove all the British and foreign community, except the large numbers of Indians, Pakistanis and Somalis who would not be in danger, and to leave no Embassy behind. We knew we were cliff-hanging until the end and that the atmosphere might still change to open hostility, if the negotiations broke down.

In the event, we were able to hand over a skeleton Embassy staff to the protection of the Arab army, which gave us assurances that they would look after all foreigners. The Embassy could not be formally established until there was a Government which could be recognised and to which the Embassy could be accredited. The remaining British and other foreign civilians chose to stay. Although neither side gave way on the Kuria Murias, agreement was reached at Geneva, with a promise of £12 million of aid for the first six months after independence, a commitment to negotiate on further aid after that and firm assurances that the new Government would protect foreigners and their property. The NLF, now in sight of power and needing money, had the sense to come to terms. There had been so many conferences about the future of South Arabia. All had broken down. Now at last in a few days under pressure of events one succeeded. If there had been more time, it would probably have failed too. In New York the impotent United Nations Mission, a sort of 'Mad Hatter's tea-party', issued their report, accusing. the British of various delinquencies. No one read it. Events had passed it by.

When I arrived, the burning issue had been the detainees and the emergency regulations. As it turned out, we released batches of detainees successively at our convenience, until they were all gone, the last of the hard core FLOSY terrorists being shipped out to Cairo by the International Red Cross, to prevent their being killed by the NLF. A few days before we left, we repealed the emergency legislation in our own time and on our own initiative, substituting for it terminal legislation more suited to the last days of our stay. We flew out the remaining intelligence officers who might have been the target of released terrorists. We had acted as it suited us and had never given in to pressure from political groups inside and outside the country to release the detainees and dismantle the legislation by which they were held.

In the last few days of our stay I had the honour of reviewing the considerable fleet now collected in Aden to cover the evacuation. On 28 November the Commander-in-Chief and I left, being seen off at the airport by senior officers of the Arab army and police and by Arab civil servants, while the military band, to the delight of the Press, played 'Fings ain't what they used to be'. On 29 November the last British troops left. It all happened in perfect peace. The G.O.C. left last in a helicopter which nearly ran out of petrol on the way to the ship. The staff of the embryo Embassy, all volunteers, went back to it. It must have been a nervous moment, though a Commando carrier was left in the neighbourhood for some time, ready to pull out the foreigners, should things go wrong. On the next day, President Qahtan as Sha'abi and his delegation returned to Aden in a chartered aircraft, scheduled to touch down nowhere in the Middle East except either Beirut or Asmara. They still did not trust the Egyptians. The local boys had made good, without the taint of British or Egyptian connivance. The People's Republic of South Yemen was born, without friends, with only a promise of temporary aid and with indigenous resources to meet no more than a third of the previous level of expenditure.

7

I n the eleven months of 1967 during which we were still in Aden, 44 British soldiers and 9 British civilians had been killed, 337 soldiers and 34 civilians wounded. British Forces had killed 119 Arabs and wounded 123. Statistics of Arabs killed by Arabs were difficult to collect. The dead and wounded were taken off quickly during the fighting between the factions and were often not brought to hospital. We estimated that in the same period the dead in this fighting amounted to about 250 and the wounded to about 800, but the numbers may have been considerably larger. I cannot too highly commend the British troops employed on their unpleasant task. No other army in the world would have conducted themselves with such firmness, restraint and discipline. British civilians, men and women, carried out their duties in dangerous and unpleasant conditions with courage and efficiency.

We had some bad luck, particularly the mutiny of 20 June, but some good luck also, notably the withdrawal of the Egyptians from the Yemen. Our principal difficulties were that there was no cohesive and united nationalist movement with which we could negotiate, but only opposing parties fighting each other as well as us and unwilling to negotiate until one had come out on top, that the Arab army was similarly split and that the legitimate Government was too weak to survive. There was a background of continual tribal warfare and a real threat of anarchy, which still remains. How far this situation was caused by mistaken policies in the past, it was not for me to judge. I came in at the end, with the precise task to conduct our withdrawal and, if possible, to leave the country in peace.

A British civil servant who had worked devotedly in the Federation since its inception and had been for eleven years in South Arabia, afterwards wrote to me: 'During my wanderings I have frequently cogitated about our last months in South Arabia, and I believe we were much closer to a major disaster than is generally appreciated . . . At any time in the weeks immediately after you assumed charge, a massacre of British civilians could have taken place which would have led to an outright collision between the British and South Arabian Forces. We were within a trigger-pressure of such a calamity on the 20 June. We might then have found ourselves sucked into a Vietnam-type situation leading after much bloodshed to a fighting withdrawal and, in the process, the destruction of Aden. Because the evacuation took place without a disaster, people may never fully appreciate the dangers of the situation in South Arabia from the outbreak of the Arab-Israeli war onwards . . . When one remembers the position in the last week of June with Crater under siege . . . the Arab army in a state of near-mutiny, a hundred British soldiers and civilians virtual hostages up-country, another hundred British officials in the power of the Arab Forces at Ittihad (the Federal capital), and the British commercial community scattered throughout the colony, one realises how near we were to calamity.' So we left without glory but without disaster. Nor was it humiliation. For our withdrawal was the result not of military or political pressure but of our decision, right or wrong, to leave, and if we failed to hand over our colony in the manner which we should have wished, it was principally because the South Arabians were unable to produce in time a responsible political party having the support of the majority of the people and prepared to negotiate a more civilised approach to independence.

The political problem, fencing with a vacuum, had its fascination. There were moments of real distress, which I still feel, the murder of a young man who was doing his job with efficiency and sympathy for those who shot him, the murder of other civilians caught up in a quarrel which was none of their concern, the fate of the soldiers ambushed in Crater on 20 June, the murder of the two men who were helping a young Ruler in trouble to return to his home, the deaths of others engaged in helping the people who killed them. All we could say at the time was that it might have been much worse. And, in the end, another little independent Arab country came into being, desperately poor and probably destined to go through periods of violence and revolt. The mark of the British on it was light and will soon have disappeared save for the great barracks, the airport, the disused churches and a few half-obliterated direction signs to the NAAFI or the sergeants' mess. Our period of occupation did the country little permanent good, for all the selfless work of many devoted Englishmen and so many good intentions. Whatever the rights or wrongs of the way we left, whatever was to come after us, the time for us to be there was over. And if we were to go, it was better not to linger on.

INDEX

INDEX

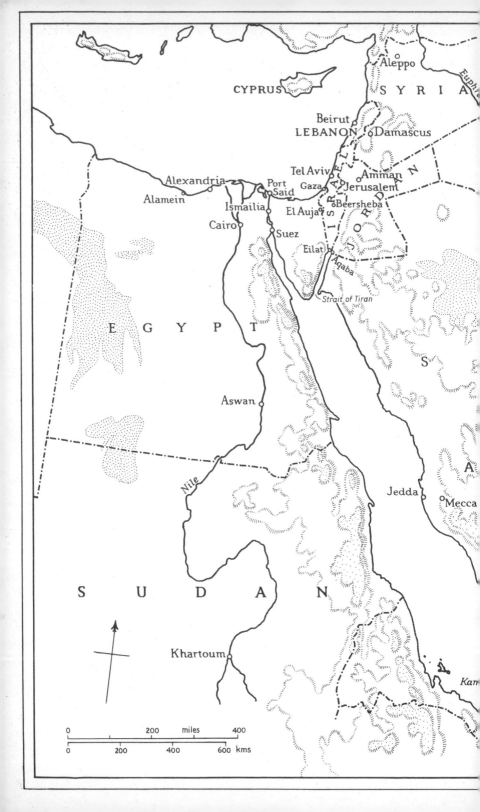